PORNO-GRAPHICS & PORNO-TACTICS

BEFORE YOU START TO READ THIS BOOK, take this moment to think about making a donation to punctum books, an independent non-profit press,

@ https://punctumbooks.com/support/

If you're reading the e-book, you can click on the image below to go directly to our donations site. Any amount, no matter the size, is appreciated and will help us to keep our ship of fools afloat. Contributions from dedicated readers will also help us to keep our commons open and to cultivate new work that can't find a welcoming port elsewhere. Our adventure is not possible without your support.
Vive la open-access.

Fig. 1. Hieronymus Bosch, *Ship of Fools* (1490–1500)

PORNO-GRAPHICS & PORNO-TACTICS: DESIRE, AFFECT, AND REPRESENTATION IN PORNOGRAPHY. Copyright © 2016 Editors and authors. This work carries a Creative Commons BY-NC-SA 4.0 International license, which means that you are free to copy and redistribute the material in any medium or format, and you may also remix, transform, and build upon the material, as long as you clearly attribute the work to the authors and editors (but not in a way that suggests the authors or punctum books endorses you and your work), you do not use this work for commercial gain in any form whatsoever, and that for any remixing and transformation, you distribute your rebuild under the same license. http://creativecommons.org/licenses/by-nc-sa/4.0/

First published in 2016 by punctum books, Earth, Milky Way.
www. punctumbooks.com

ISBN-13: 978-0692720547
ISBN-10: 0692720545
Library of Congress Cataloging Data is available from the Library of Congress

Book design: Vincent W.J. van Gerven Oei & Natalia Tuero
Cover image: Tejal Shah, *Lucid Dreaming V* (2013)
Tejal Shah (b. 1979, Bhilai, India; currently lives in Goa, India) graduated with a BA in photography from RMIT, Melbourne, spent a year as an exchange student at The Art Institute of Chicago and another summer trying to get an MFA from Bard College in upstate New York. Their* practice incorporates everything and anything, including video, photography, performance, food, drawing, sound, installation, and modes of sustainable living. Queerying everything, they often unselfconsciously manifest "the inappropriate/d other" – one whom you cannot appropriate and one who is inappropriate. Experiencing their works entails entering alter-curious worlds riddled with fact, fiction, poetry, and mythology, that compel us to engage with layered propositions on the relationships between interspecies, ecology, gender, post-porn, sexuality, and consciousness. Having recently come out as an ecosexual, they think of themselves as "some kind of artist working on some kind of nature."
www.tejalshah.in

Porno-Graphics & Porno-Tactics

*Desire, Affect, and Representation
in Pornography*

Edited by
Eirini Avramopoulou
& Irene Peano

CONTENTS

Challenging Pornography, Challenged by Pornography:
From Monstrous Tactics to Enactments of *Poiēsis*
    Eirini Avramopoulou and Irene Peano · · · · · · · · · · · · · · · · · 13

Interview with Émilie Jouvet
    Eirini Avramopoulou, Irene Peano, and Adele Tulli · · · · · · · ·29

Open Letter on Empowerment and Queer Porn
    Kathryn Fischer ·39

A Seductive Intrigue of Sexuality?
    Sinan Goknur ·45

Everyday Porn
    Namita Aavriti ·51

Look! But Also, Touch!: Theorizing Images of Trans Eroticism
Beyond a Politics of Visual Essentialism
    Eliza Steinbock ·59

Pornography for Blind and Visually Impaired People:
On Tactility and Monstrosity
    Elia Charidi ·77

A Note on Pornography and Violence
    Mantas Kvedaravicius ·85

Biographies ·95

DEDICATIONS AND ACKNOWLEDGMENTS

This book is dedicated to sex, love and friendship.

A number of people helped us through this creative and inspiring period, during which we worked to bring together this edited volume. First of all, we want to thank all contributors for their energy, ideas and patience in the process of publishing this. Adele Tulli was, as always, a friend and fundamental inspiring presence throughout. Previous drafts of these essays were initially collected for publication at the Re-public online platform, which unfortunately had to be discontinued due to financial reasons. We would like to thank the managing editors, and particularly Pavlos Hatzopoulos, for making the assemblage and publication of the first collection possible. At punctum books, we are grateful to Eileen A. Joy for her enthusiastic and unrelenting support, and to Vincent W.J. van Gerven Oei and Natalia Tuero for their fantastic editorial work. Our gratitude also goes to Elena Loizidou for her precious and acute comments, to Clarrie Pope for an equally scrupulous and timely proofreading (which went well beyond the task), to Evelina Gambino for her help with bibliographic references in one of the chapters, and to Tejal Shah for agreeing to share their fantastic artwork for the book cover.

Challenging Pornography, Challenged by Pornography: From Monstrous Tactics to Enactments of *Poiēsis*

Eirini Avramopoulou and Irene Peano

1. Beginnings

The point of departure of this edited volume was experimental, and so too is its result. The idea for this collection initially sprung from a need, not to mention desire, to open up, relate to and test the limits of certain avenues of thought and their material implications. These were part of our intellectual horizons and everyday experiences when we were living in the UK, but were also shaped by our moving in and out of the country, and through friends, or friends of friends, families of all kinds, comrades, books, objects, concepts etc. from all over the world. The idea came from a need to experiment with (familiar or unfamiliar) others, so as to create a platform of engagement while "sweating" with certain concepts, as Sarah Ahmed so beautifully put it.[1] But such need to experiment derived from the fact that we had already found ourselves "sweating" with desire in our everyday lives, in relationships that

---

[1] Sara Ahmed, "Changing hands: Some Reflections on Ann Oakley's *Sex, Gender and Society*," presented at the *Revisiting Feminist Classics Symposium*, Cambridge University, 2013. http://feministkilljoys.com/2013/08/28/changing-hands/.

were confronting us with our own failed attempts to transcend limits, in feelings of embarrassment, frustration, and anger with imposed structures, in repeating what we had promised ourselves never to do again, in blushing with guilt for something we never for a moment thought we would do, but at the same time feeling the liberation of doing it, in not admitting to ourselves and others that queer might not be the word to define all of our unreleased fantasies, or in asking what the limits of queer might be... – the list of our meanderings in the realms of desire and sexuality could go on endlessly.

Indeed, as Sarah Ahmed writes,[2] concepts emerge out of bodies and they return to those bodies. Put differently, concepts are worked through "in the flesh" to make sense of our lived experiences and different realities, of our censored pleasures and closeted desires. Thinking through pornography, then, entails re-engaging with the question of desire – as this redefines identity claims, embodied acts, and intersubjective encounters, but also as it encircles our different affective responses to practices and politics in everyday life. When this project was first conceived, we thought it necessary to experiment with the ways in which we think of, write, imagine, and perform our sexualities in attempts to traverse, or even subvert, normative inscriptions, while knowing that this is no simple job.

Re-appropriating pornography, or at least questioning the possibility of doing so and thinking through it, becomes a way, then, to re-articulate aporias of desire, intimacy, touch, and seduction. These are related, but not restricted, to claims of visibility, visions of emancipation and its failure, as well as to the politics of violence that we are exposed to through circulating images and affects, augmenting or confining us. In other words, expressing such aporias represents an attempt to exceed the limits set by and for ourselves in relation to how we connect to our own bodies, to the bodies of our lovers and to the bodies of the theories we live with, sleep with, and dream about – in short, to all that we get attached to.

---

2   Ibid.

Hence, the very subject of these embodied reflections makes them so eminently intimate, personal but never individual – and this is true not just of our own engagement, but of that of the many contributors to this collection. Reflexivity as a political stance is a common thread running through several chapters in this book, a lesson learned from feminism and remodulated through contemporary struggles over boundaries and their excesses, refusals, and overcomings. Indeed, many of the texts in this volume emerge from personal experiences and experiments, and in this sense they reflect the complex processes of *elaborating* and *enacting* the theory that one embraces, i.e., the processes of feelings and sensations, performative actions and discursive positions, past experiences and future expectations, social norms and political identifications transmitted to and affected by the need for "releasing desire."

Judith Butler asks how we can conceive of an erotic togetherness "released from" a hegemonic heteronormativity,[3] and concludes: "It seems to me that sexuality is always returning to the binds from which it seeks to release, and so perhaps follows a different kind of rhythm and temporality than most emancipatory schemes would suggest."[4] How can we follow this rhythm and let ourselves be deranged by it? These contributions attempt to answer this question by challenging boundaries, and by failing to abide by any straightforward distinction between analysis and performance, or between art, politics, and academia. They refuse to be restricted to any particular domain.

Moreover, it is important to consider points of departure as they both reveal our own rootedness as well as the routes one takes to reach certain destinations. Following feminist activist gatherings, participating in queer groups and at the same time having endless discussions about the constraints of gender, the limits of sexuality, and the performative potential of being and doing "it" otherwise, in the context of a renewed interest in pornography and its re-appropriation by queer performers, activists, and intel-

---

3   Athena Athanasiou and Judith Butler, *Dispossession: The Performative in the Political* (Cambridge & Malden: Polity Press 2013), 53.
4   Ibid., 54.

lectuals, we were constantly stumbling over the same question: is pornography as a concept and practice something worth thinking through again, sweating with again, getting excited about again, sleeping with again? Questions that sparked off our fragmented discussions were as simple as: Do you watch porn? What makes you feel aroused in sex? What do the images that circulate do to us and to our desires? How have desire and sexuality been oppressed, and why do they continue to feel oppressive? How do you claim liberation? Or how can one reclaim images of sexual desire if through our feminist lenses we cannot help but scrutinize, mock, and even feel disgusted by the repetitive representations of a male, heteronormative, and white gaze and the market economy of pleasure that sustains it and is sustained by it?

These questions led to what has now emerged as a deliberately heterogeneous, non-canonic collection of short essays. Our positive answer to whether pornography, as a concept or practice, is worth reconsidering echoed both feminist criticism, which always helps us to be alert to whatever might be mirrored in or through the embodied fantasies of a male-driven hegemony of pleasure, as well as the need to feel the difference in what queer theorists have been trying to transmit to us by locating and dislocating the object–subject of desire, lust, and pleasure through images, bodies, objects, and performances that exceed certain established limits of representation, perception, and intelligibility.

2. *From Monstrous Tactics to Enactments of* Poiēsis

Of course, since the 1970s, pornography's inscriptions have troubled feminist writers, who have been critically addressing issues related to the representation of the female body. Porn, it was contended, is for the most part a heterosexist (and often racist) genre, and its market circulation serves male arousal alone, fixing the position of pleasure for both wo/men and abiding by patriarchal norms. A strand of feminism, headed by Catharine Mackinnon and Andrea Dworkin, called for the banning of pornography, arguing that it harmed women by objectifying (and thus de-subjectifying) them.[5] Others, like Judith Butler,[6] Lauren Berlant,[7] and Drucilla Cornell,[8] have argued that the depiction of sex can be empowering to women, and others still, like Carl Stychin,[9] have made analogous comments about gay pornography. Yet, equally "sex positive" critics have also employed the term in a critical way, understanding it metonymically as "a system of representation that reinforces the profit-making logic of the capitalist market economy."[10] According to this perspective, the serial repetition of scenes typical of pornography as of other genres and forms of representation (most notably advertising), by titillating desire and at the same time frustrating its fulfillment, creates that generalized form of addiction which characterizes consumer society. Braidotti depicts pornography as the production of "images without imagination" based on a "logistics of representation" centered on the subject-object dichotomy, in turn predicated on a power relation.[11]

These thinkers conceive of pornography as a gaze upon different others, in which race, religion, and class come to the forefront alongside gender and sexuality. From Braidotti who addresses issues of racism in Islamophobic representations such as the documentary *Fitna,* or the "medical pornography" of fetal images detached from the mother's body for the purpose of anti-abortion campaigns, to the many commentators who relate pornography

5 Cf. for example Andrea Dworkin, Pornography: *Men Possessing Women* (London: Women's Press, 1981); Catherine Mackinnon, *Toward a Feminist Theory of the State* (Cambridge, MA: Harvard University Press, 1989); Dworkin, "Against the Male Flood: Censorship, Pornography, and Equality," in C. Itzin (ed.), *Pornography: Woman, Violence and Civil Liberties* (Oxford: Oxford University Press, 1994), 515–35; Dworkin and Mackinnon, *In Harm's Way: The Pornography Civil Rights Hearings* (Cambridge, MA: Harvard University Press, 1997).
6 Judith Butler, "The Force of Fantasy: Feminism, Mapplethorpe, and Discursive Excess," *Journal of Feminist Cultural Studies* 2, no. 2 (1990): 105–25.
7 Lauren Berlant, "Live Sex Acts," *Feminist Studies* 21, no. 2 (1995): 379–404.
8 Drucilla Cornell, *The Imaginary Domain* (New York: Routledge. 1995).
9 Carl Stychin, *Law's desire: Sexuality and the Limits of Justice* (New York: Routledge, 1995).
10 Rosi Braidotti, *Nomadic Subjects: Embodiment and Sexual Difference in Contemporary Feminist Theory,* 2nd ed. (New York: Columbia University Press, 2011), 68, after Kappelar's 1986 *The Pornography of Representation.*
11 Ibid.

to acts of torture, most notably in Abu Ghraib,[12] pornography becomes a "concept metaphor" used to denounce different processes of violent subjectification. Likewise, horror-like depictions of what has come to be known as "sex trafficking" have been denounced for their voyeuristic tendency to prey on aprioristically assumed and defined forms of suffering, that supposedly arouse humanitarian affective responses.[13] A twisted, prudish morality comes full circle in both decrying and feeding off suffering and sexual exploitation.

On the other hand, many newly emerging artworks, documentaries, and porn productions attempt to exscribe from porn its initial, normatively repressive qualities, and re-inscribe a feminist or queer perception of enjoyment and pleasure while pushing the limits of normative and normalizing representations further. In such "tactics,"[14] pornography seeks to reclaim the language (and more broadly the representation, or the enactment and transmission) of desire and pleasure so as to enable ways of questioning normative transgression, as well as to facilitate the exploration of unclaimed desires, unintelligible acts, and censored affects.

Yet, how such reclaiming might work remains an open question, given the centrality of pornography in contemporary political–economic configurations, and the fact that the commercial aspect of pornography is deeply embedded in its genealogy (literally, the term means "writing about prostitutes", where the Greek term for prostitute, *pornē*, means "purchased"). In the current era, which Beatriz (now Paul) Preciado baptized as "farmacopornographic,"[15] the governmental and industrial management of sexuality and the body dominate (at least in some corners of the planet). The cri-

---

12 Anne McClintock, "Paranoid Empire: Specters from Guantánamo and Abu Ghraib, *Small Axe* 28, no. 1 (2009): 50–74.
13 Cf., for example, Joan Lindquist, "Images and Evidence: Human Trafficking, Auditing, and the Production of Illicit Markets in Southeast Asia and Beyond," *Public Culture* 22, no. 2 (2010): 223–36.
14 Michel de Certeau, *The Practice of Everyday Life* (Berkeley: University of California Press, 1984).
15 Beatriz Preciado, *Testo Junkie: Sex, Drugs and Biopolitics in the Pharmacopornographic Era* (New York: The Feminist Press, 2008).

tique of pornography is thus brought to a new level, which considers it not only as a system of representation (like those works we previously evoked) but as a form of production and control of bodies, affects, and desires. Preciado perceptively observes that capital puts to work the potential for sexual excitation, or "orgasmic force,"[16] through cycles of pharmacological, pornographic, or sexual-service production and consumption. This kind of extraction exceeds heteronormative boundaries, subject–object distinctions, forms of racialization, applying instead to "the living pansexual body", which thereby becomes "the bioport" of orgasmic force and is thus located at the juncture of production and culture, which "belongs to technoscience."[17]

If, Preciado observes, "[t]echnobodies are either not-yet-alive or already-dead"; if "we are half fetuses, half zombies," then "every politics of resistance is a monster politics."[18] Elsewhere,[19] they had referred to monstrosity as unrepresentable difference, arguing that it is from this position, that of the "abnormals," that a creative reappropriation of and through bodies, spaces, and sexual politics becomes possible. In many ways, their advocacy of monstrosity builds on earlier reflections on the theme, most notably by Donna Haraway and Rosi Braidotti.[20]

Indeed, we can read terato-political tendencies in many contributions to this volume. From the trans movies that Eliza Steinbock analyzes to the (more problematic but nonetheless provocative) pornographic magazines for the visually impaired scrutinized by Elia Charidi, we are challenged to think of new, monstrous

16 Ibid., 41–50.
17 Ibid., 43.
18 Ibid., 44.
19 Beatriz Preciado, "Multitudes queer: Notes pour une politique des 'anormaux,'" *Multitudes* 2, no. 12 (2003), 17–25.
20 Donna Haraway, "The Promises of Monsters: A Regenerative Politics for Inappropriate/d Others," in Lawrence Grossberg, Cary Nelson, Paula A. Treichler (eds), *Cultural Studies* (New York: Routledge, 1992), 295–337; Rosi Braidotti, "Signs of Wonder and Traces of Doubt: On Teratology and Embodied Differences," in N. Lykke & R. Braidotti (eds), *Between Monsters, Goddesses and Cyborgs: Feminist Confrontations with Science, Medicine and Cyberspace* (London & New Jersey: Zed Books, 1996), 135–52.

configurations of bodies and desires that (partly) challenge the control of orgasmic force and its channeling along specific lines that define gender, sexuality, ability etc. In many of the essays, inappropriate/d, monstrous, abnormal characters defy identity and stable body configurations.

In this vein, instead of returning to the location of the body and its identity as a point of departure for reflection and politics (as woman, lesbian, black person, worker, subaltern, or the inhabitant of an "impaired" body), many proponents of postpornographic performance have drawn our attention to what is enabled by desire, as an affect that escapes signification and has the potential to reshuffle established ideas, morals, norms, and stereotypes. Put differently, while using the lenses of desire reminds us how human bodies have become materialized and de-materialized through histories of oppression, violence, slavery, colonization, commodification, gender, and sexual normativity, as well as through secular theology and securitarian governmentality, it also helps us to depart from any strict and stationary origin. As Elspeth Probyn argues:

> Freeing desire from its location, its epistemological stake, in the individual necessitates rethinking the role of images, images and motion. For the queer image does indeed express something. From this intuition, it then becomes a question of how to express the singularity of queer desire, of how to queer the movement of images in a singular way.[21]

Dislocating the body from a fixed subject position and opening it up to its intersubjective encounters might also be seen as a moment of *poiēsis*. As Athanasiou and Butler remind us,[22] moments of (self-)*poiēsis* carry the potential to de-institute the classifications through which identities are institutionalized and naturalized and

---

21 Elspeth Probyn, "Queer Belongings: The Politics of Departure," in E. Grosz & E. Probyn (eds), *Sexy Bodies: The Strange Carnalities of Feminism* (London & New York: Routledge, 1995), 1–18, at 9.
22 Athanasiou and Butler, *Dispossession*.

hence resist the reiteration of images and e-motions defined and constrained by liberal imaginaries and heterosexual normativity. Such are the moments that one can find in the work of performers and artists who try to resist established norms and structures. Pornography's promise, then, appears negotiated in and through this double bind, one that is mirrored in the texts (and the artworks they refer to) put together for this experimental book.

3. Challenging Pornography's Challenges

A number of female/queer pornographers are experimenting with whether and how we can re-appropriate pornography in attempts to initiate different worlds of sensation, cultures of pleasure, bodily intimacies, and scenes of seduction. In many contributions to this collection that deal with alternative forms of pornographic representation, dreams and the imagination are central elements. The work of director Emilie Jouvet, interviewed for this collection by Adele Tulli and the editors, is a prominent example of such orientation. In her work, the camera captures encounters that are moments of creative experimentation, indeed of self-*poiēsis*: there are no scripts, and collaboration between director and performers is essential. Here, orgasmic force is released outside commercial channels and prescribed roles.

What is more, the monsters produced and embodied by post-pornographic performance also challenge one of the core axes on which mainstream pornography founds its normative power: that of vision, of the "scopic drive" that, many analysts have pointed out, serves as a form of domination.[23] Indeed, in the essays by Eliza Steinbock, Namita Aavriti, and Sinan Goknur, in particular, the synesthetic link between the tactile and the visual is emphasized, thus moving representation beyond the visual to reflect on the circulation of affect and the power of touch, but also on the power of hiding, on what is withheld or cannot be seen. The porno-tactical, then, is also porno-tactile.

23 Cf. Braidotti, *Nomadic Subjects*, 66–74.

On the other hand, the promise of the politics of performativity – which we can read when a term is reclaimed so as to re-produce it in difference – always defines the premise of possible misfire.[24] Similarly, desire conceived as a liberating and transcendental "line of flight" might get stuck in our own rootedness, which could hold us back and make us feel immobilized when trying to evade, let alone defy, the norms and structures of everyday life. In this volume, Kathryn Fisher, an actress in queer porn and a sexually explicit performer, argues that there is nothing inherently empowering about making porn because empowerment is a process and not an end. Being part of a queer, feminist, low-budget, DIY porn movement doesn't necessarily pay your bills, and you cannot always avoid social prejudices regarding your practices and intentions. This alerts us to the pervasiveness of different modes of exploitation even in the face of attempts to resist them. Nevertheless, as Kathryn argues:

> what is really queer, really revolutionary, and really powerful, is working at relationships with each other, receiving each other with love, understanding each other, trying to find out about each other, making assumptions for the best, and supporting each other on good and bad days.

With these words, she reminds us that when empowerment becomes a process which entails breaking taboos and stereotypes that we hold about each other, and when we are able to communicate without imposing our politics and morality on others, this holds a promise of something new that might emerge from within those processes and ways of relating.

Even if most of the articles in this volume ally with Kathryn's questioning of easy accounts of emancipation, at the same time most also contain an attempt to make us think about the potentialities carried in and through the re-articulation of sexual explicitness. This also resonates, for example, with what Sinan Goknur

---

24 Judith Butler, *Excitable Speech: A Politics of the Performative* (New York: Routledge, 1997).

calls *vital seduction,* that he defines as a process, or rather a play, *between* sex and desire, and not as something rooted in either sex or desire alone. Following Baudrillard's criticism of the explicitness of sexuality in the sex industry[25] as something that demystifies desire and strips sex of its seductive aura by turning it into a banal reality, Sinan's self-reflective analysis, as a transgender person and an active advocate of sex-positive queer and feminist politics, touches upon possible misfires connected to feminist/queer visions of pleasure and to activist claims to visibility.

Considering the ways that biopolitics and governmentality get intertwined, Namita Aavriti's paper examines the effects of the insertion of amateur video porn into everyday life and the market economy in India, as well as the role of the state and the law in defining and controlling the parameters of this industry. More importantly, Namita argues that although amateur pornography enables the emergence of different affects in relation to conventional big-screen porn production, at the same time it is also part and parcel of a biopolitical process through which bodies (especially female bodies) become more readily accessible to the fantasy of touching them. Amateur pornography blurs the boundaries of what might be considered as real or fictional by making bodies available to be "touched" through gaze.

Indeed, how can we think of the process of releasing desire as a way to communicate different realities, political visions, and visual signifiers through which we can touch and be touched by each other? Or, how can one "feel desire's shimmering activity through the synesthetic modalities of touch intertwining with vision"? Eliza Steinbock asks such question in her piece, following Susan Stryker's analysis of the *spectrum of desire* to interpret it as *poiēsis* of the trans body.[26] Eliza's argument emphasizes the troubling but promising relationship between visibility and touch in trans people's embodiments, sexualities, and eroticism

25 Jean Baudrillard, "Dust Breeding," in Jean Baudrillard and Sylvère Lotringer (eds), *The Conspiracy of Art: Manifestos, Interviews, Essays* (New York: Semiotext(e), 2005), 181–88.
26 Susan Stryker, "Dungeon Intimacies: The Poetics of Transsexual Sadomasochism," *Parallax* 14, no. 1 (2008): 36–47.

that have been defined by the conflicting relationship between visibility and concealment. As she argues, "Trans pornography may cite the identity politics of visibility, but it also offers a rich opportunity for investigating the force, shape and experience of trans-eroticism through touch." However, if attempts to *look into* trans sexualities pass through the production of images that aim to assemble empirical knowledge about the *reality* of sex acts, relying on and reproducing what Eliza calls a "visual essentialism," identities of desire are once again fixed. Like Sinan and Kathryn, Eliza also questions the liberating effects of an identity politics based on visibility and argues that what is politically at stake in trans porn is that it sets in motion a process, not of reflecting, but of engendering "real" bodies, desires, and experiences both on and off the screen.

The troubling politics of touch that are analyzed in Eliza's paper are also the locus of attention in Elia Charidi's chapter on the pornography of blind people. In different but similar ways, both authors criticize the ways that bodies that do not conform to established norms and desires are either de-eroticized or hyper-eroticized. At the same time, Elia's paper implicitly challenges the limits of intersectionality – which, as Sinan argues, is nevertheless an important lens to employ in order to consider different systems and mechanisms of sexual desire and oppression together. What kinds of fantasies does the porn industry attribute to bodies that do not fit into established categories? And what would inclusion entail here? One way to provide a critical answer to these questions is to examine how sexuality and impairment come together in attempts to move away from current stereotypes of bodily beauty and the aesthetics of pleasure. Elia claims that Lisa Murphy's 2010 pornographic magazine for blind and visually impaired people, *Tactile Minds,* is such an attempt. However, Elia points out that even this fails to completely escape normative dualisms that underscore presumptions and fantasies about lack of vision, such as darkness–light, body–mind, flesh–spirit, subconsciousness–consciousness. Moreover, it is difficult to forget that being blind, as well as being sighted, is an identity built up on several stereotypes and embodied fantasies. As Nina Lykke argued long ago:

Questions of gender, race, ethnicity, sexual preference, age, and other socio- and biocultural differences and power differentials are constantly intersecting. This heterogeneity enhances the need not only for multi- and transdisciplinary approaches but also for a superimposition of different lenses of inquiry – feminist, multicultural, ecological, and so on – which can make the different elements of the heterogeneous networks become visible.[27]

If touch gives people with severe visual impairment access to a visual world of sexual representation that they had previously been deprived of, and if this is a way of seeking to emancipate and include those who had been excluded from the technology of sexual pleasure, this will only work if we keep in mind, and so challenge, the deeply embedded norms that historically haunt the impaired body. Elia points out that from Ernesto Sabado to Lisa Murphy, blindness has repeatedly been perceived as attached to the obscene and to sexual fantasies of monstrosity. As Rosi Braidotti convincingly explains:

> The monstrous body, more than an object, is a shifter, a vehicle that constructs a web of interconnected and yet potentially contradictory discourses about his or her embodied self. Gender and race are primary operators in this process.[28]

Last but not least, Mantas Kvedaravicius's paper focuses on the production of a political economy of pornographic images of rape and torture, which is difficult to access and so also difficult to analyze. Following Anne McClintock, Mantas asks how to think of, or not think of, pornography and violence together, when pleasure and pain, power and sexuality (which often seem to form a single register, for example in the cases of Abu Ghraib, Guantánamo, or Chechnya) continue to haunt everyday life. He also raises ques-

---

27 Nina Lykke, "Introduction," in Lykke & Braidotti (eds), *Between Monsters, Goddesses and Cyborgs*, 1–10.
28 Braidotti, "Signs of Wonder and Traces of Doubt," 150.

tions about our ability to provide adequate responses to this relationship. Is it possible not to think of images of penetration as the reification of coercive power, absolute domination, and moral humiliation? How not to consider the complex dynamics of race, class, gender, and sexuality that the pornographic gaze is immersed in and hence institutionalized by? How can we not think of the religious connotations embedded in the secular bodies of modernity that reproduce voyeuristic images of penetrating the other's wounds? Such explicit violence also contains something that is rendered radically unrepresentable for Mantas, whose writings try to inscribe and at the same time erase such effects. Thinking self-reflectively about the (im)possibility of writing or speaking about the explicitness of violent sexualized acts, Mantas asks whether we can, through our writings, transmit an image of the other without repeating moralistic claims, and most of all without naively affirming liberation, especially when the techniques and technologies that we use to seek emancipation are embedded in their own violent histories of domination. As he asks, "What kind of regime of representation does the repetition of banality of violence and the obscene include?"

The authors in this collection reflect on pornography from the point of view both of the "politics of representation," which it may apply, subvert, reproduce, and perform, and also of its "affective and libidinal" dimensions. Without claiming the euphoric potentiality of pornography as necessarily subversive and emancipatory, the papers open up possibilities for re-writing (in textual, contextual, intertextual, but also affective and embodied forms) about pornography through different graphic and tactical/tactile inscriptions.

Therefore, on the one hand the contributors reflect on definitions and practices of pornography as a genre adopting specific codes and canons, whether narrowly conceived as those concerned with sex acts and the porn industry or more broadly with other predominant forms of representation, fantasies and imaginaries. They ask: Can "pornography" be used in an untroubled way, or without questioning its initial inscription as a normative vision of representation *per se* and other forms of (embodied, inter/subjective) desire? How easy is it to reclaim it as a term? What would this entail? To what extent are discursive forms efficacious in shaping subjectivities, and how might we understand their failures and excesses? What might pornographic representations conceal?

These questions intersect with the second aspect of pornography as experience, in its affective, libidinal, inter/subjective dimensions. How does the affective intersect with the symbolic? Where, if anywhere, lies the potential for pornographic experience and representation to subvert existing mechanisms of subjection? And what kind of economic, (bio)political deployments do representations and affects intersect with?

The papers published in this volume tackle these questions from different standpoints in more or less direct ways. We hope they will foster further reflections on issues of representation, affect, sex and sexuality, desire and pleasure, art, academia, and engagement.

Interview with Émilie Jouvet

Eirini Avramopoulou, Irene Peano, and Adele Tulli

What is pornography for you? Do you consider your work pornographic, or how does your work relate to activist-oriented, feminist/queer porn productions (what is usually referred to as "post-porn")?

Pornography is representing an explicit sexual act. However, it's not my job to produce it, others do it very well, on a large scale and in a stylish way, like Shine Louise Houston or Courtney Trouble. Each artist has her own way of working and her own aesthetics. There are movements and currents of thought, which evolve in time and sometimes contradict each other. Personally, I don't really like the term "post" (post-porn, post-feminism…), nor do I feel represented by the term "queer artist."

I am a French visual artist who expresses herself through photography, contemporary video, and cinema. I am a militant feminist, lesbian, and queer. I take pictures of and film my female friends in moments of intimacy, during parties, and in everyday life. My models are often queer; they are writers, feminists, militants, DJs, femme, dykes, or butch lesbians, trans, etc. My first contact with the queer scene dates back to the beginning of the 2000s, where as a very young artist I was part of a collective of artists called Queer Factory, a collective of queer, lesbian, gay, bi, or trans authors and creators, adhering to the subversive value of creation in all its forms. But I do not make "queer art" nor "post-porn." As any artist, what I say and show is born out of my mental and physical experiments with exterior and interior, it is a representation of the world through the prism of my identity, and vice versa.

My sources of inspiration are literary, feminist, artistic, pornographic, punk, dyke, and self-fictional. My personal "creative energy" is built out of sisterhood, nostalgia, rebellion, the fear of death, solitude, love/passion, hunger, desire, politics, rage, complicity, and sex. I feel close to the work of the director, visual artist, and musician Sadie Benning and to her exploration of sexual identity, the use and subversion of pop-culture images, of which she said: "They are completely false and constructed to divert and oppress at the same time. They don't make any sense for women [in general], and not only for lesbians. I decided to start shooting in part because I needed other images and I never wanted to wait for others to do it for me." I was also very inspired by artists such as Orlan, Barbara Kruger, Gina Pane, Catherine Opie, Kiki Smith, Hannah Wilke, The Guerilla Girls, Dyke Action Machine... The works of writers and theoreticians such as Monique Wittig, Audre Lorde, Dorothy Allison, Virginie Despentes were equally important in my personal trajectory.

So why represent sex?

In my work sexuality is a space of thought and creativity. I have sometimes shown representations of desire and the sexual acts of people whose gender or sexuality is usually disparaged, made invisible, or silenced. The representation of sex, in art or cinema, is as important as other subjects. I don't like there to be a hierarchy. I am particularly interested in the sex-positive feminist movement, or pro-sex feminism, which in the United States of the 1980s opened the way for the reappropriation of women's bodies and sexuality, and of their representations.

I work against the sexism and puritanism that are omnipresent in our societies. In my photos and films, I like to interrogate contemporary taboos concerning the human body and to work on the way in which we perceive them. The aesthetics of my images differs from fashion magazine pictures or mainstream pornography. I try to give voice (and vision) to those people who hold an alternative discourse. I have become convinced that sexuality is one of the strategic sites for the oppression of women (even if the oppression of women is far from being limited to sexuality). The biggest taboo is not sex, it's the words (and images) of women and minorities on sex. It's also speaking about violence, denouncing censorship, unveiling the mechanisms that make us [women] individuals with less liberties and rights.

The artists I film in the road-movie documentary *Too Much Pussy, Feminist Sluts in the Queer X Show* put forth ideas about sexuality and freedom that are very specific and are part of a sex-positive feminism. In *Too Much Pussy* the erotic scenes, in which one understands that the artists on the tour have sexual adventures, are part of the narrative structure of the film. I wanted to show sexuality in different ways: in its representation on the stage (the show), in its political aspect (the big discussions on the road, between each show), but also real sexuality, in intimate situations. These three axes are dealt with as part of the same prism, as different facets of the same question, that of sexual freedom.

If resistance and transgression are present, it is as a woman's gaze on women's discourses and bodies, a gaze that gives other women power and the capacity to speak, whereas mainstream cinema has generally accustomed us to a rather objectifying male gaze. This film is above all an ode to freedom, to creation, to travel, and to friendship. Freedom can be sexual, but it is also the freedom to love, as we like, whom we like. It is also the freedom not to have sex. That of not wanting to play the game of seduction. Beyond the question of sex and together with it, what I want to show is the joy, the freedom of being able to create together. If, after having seen the movie, one knows where the neck of the uterus is, how rage can transform itself into creativity, shame into pride, and the desire to be fancied into the pleasure of sharing, it's a nice thing.

The political and anti-conformist representation of multiple non-conventional femininities becomes very visible and embraced. The sexually suggestive details of some of my pictures or film scenes are conceived in terms of codes, "signs" of lesbian and queer sexuality. The work of corporeal identity proper to each model is valorized: the haircuts, the unusual postures, body modifications, boys' jeans, vests, Converse shoes, blood-red lipstick, outrageous makeup, inside-out underwear, hairiness, exhibited sex toys, the provoking postures of bodies and gazes are as many codes to mark their [the models'] erotic territory.

I had already worked on the issue of sexuality and of pornography as a very specific system of representation at the time of my studies at the beaux arts and at the national school of photography. I used to shoot videos and pictures on the subversion of objects or acts. For example, in the video *BlancX,* you can see me while I am brushing my teeth... with a vibrator. This subverted and ridiculed the classical pornographic representation of fellatio through an ordinary act. It was funny (especially for girls) and at the same time very provocative for some (the director of an art gallery exclaimed: "Here's another one who doesn't swallow!"). Also when I was a student, I wanted to do my internship on a porn movie shoot. I had wanted for a long time to see how the representations, the images of straight sexuality were constructed live. On another level, being a lesbian, having discovered that all representations of lesbians were compared to pornography, even if they weren't meant as such, this irritated me. Moreover, I realized that as lesbians we hardly ever have access to any images of sexuality that really represent us (images created by ourselves, for ourselves). Most of the time, porn movies represent a male fantasy applied to women. I don't have anything against that, but it's not at all representative.

When I saw for the first time lesbian porn made by women for women – I was 20, it was at *Cineffable* – it struck me deeply. At first, I was very shocked to finally see in these images what it could mean, what lesbian sexuality could be. We are so unfamiliar with it that it seemed just horrible. However, at the end of the night, even if everybody had hated it and declared themselves very shocked, not at all aroused, etc., in the end everybody went crazy and all the girls ended the night snogging each other and sleeping together. I told myself, there you go, we can say it's horrible but actually in the end it sort of works, you see?

Overall, I seek neither to conform to mainstream pornography, nor to exaggerate the non-conforming traits of the bodies and sexualities that I present. The people in my circle whom I film or take pictures of do not necessarily conform to the horizon of erotic expectations, straight or mainstream, of those who only appreciate women's sexual emancipation when it fits their libido, and only theirs. Rather, my models embody so many Liliths and Riot grrrls who refuse to submit to the patriarchal desire that produces the feminine sex as a weak sex.

How do the acts you represent emerge? As a director, do you leave your characters free to perform the sex scenes the way they like (you capture desire) or do you direct your characters in performing scenes you have imagined (you create desire)…? Can you describe the making of the sex scenes you have shot?

I leave my characters free to perform the sex scene. Actually, they don't really perform as actors, most of the time they just have sex and I shoot them in a documentary style. For example, *Too Much Pussy* is a road-movie documentary, and *Much More Pussy* is a film in which I gathered together all the sex scenes that took place during the tour. In *Much More Pussy* sexualities and sexual fantasies are very diverse: sex on a piano, in a ruined building, in some room… We shift from a very sensual two-way scene to a really intense six-way group scene, a fisting scene, we can see very beautiful female ejaculations, fellatios on a dildo, anal practices between women, and above all some real orgasms!

The girls were ok with me filming their sexual identity during the tour, the principle being never to impose staged "sex scenes" on the actresses, but for the girls to choose themselves, freely, their sexual partners and their practices. At the beginning of the shooting, because of the frantic work rhythm of the tour, I thought that perhaps there would be no sex scenes in the film. But the exact opposite happened! The girls had a very intense sex life, among themselves or after casual encounters, and at times it was hard for me to keep pace. For example, I remember some funny moments when, exhausted, thinking I could finally pack up my cameras and go to sleep, one or the other girl would come to find me so that I could film their progress... At the time of the editing of *Much More Pussy*, I was adamant not to censor any scene, since the principle of sex-positive feminism is also to respect others' sexual desires, not to judge or hierarchize different practices, even if they are not to our taste or if we don't understand them. Among consenting adults, the possibilities are multiple, and I have to say that I was often surprised to discover such diversity and creativity in the sexual adventures of each person. I learned a lot, both about different practices and about my own prejudices. In 2011 the use of sex toys, s/M practices, or bondage among girls are unfortunately still the object of debate for certain people ready to judge and moralize others' practices.

What dictates the choice of DIY (Do It Yourself) production?

DIY is not a choice, it's the sad reality: mainstream production companies are afraid to give money for such unconventional and subversive projects (something like a mixture of feminism, queer theory, and sexuality)!

Too Much Pussy was self-funded for the most part. It took us a year to gather enough money between us to be able to leave for the tour and make the film. I had to stop working for two years and dedicate myself entirely to the film. Like the majority of militant films that never obtain any public funding or big production budgets, this film was made under DIY conditions, without a shooting crew, sleeping in people's places, etc. Over a year of work persevering through self-management and self-production. Around a hundred artists and friends took part (transporting and making the scenery and props, driving the van in the tour, making costumes, creating music, finding sponsors and people to accommodate the team in five different countries). We organized several benefit nights in Paris and Berlin. Two friends, who are alternative co-producers from Paris and Berlin, helped us with the renting of the van and the kit. Loads of new people we met every day supported the project day by day during the tour. It was the most exciting, but also the most exhausting cinematographic experience of my whole life. Shooting without the traditional financial support is like making a "mutilated" but free film.

There is little consideration for that art which lives outside traditional circuits. We still live on the myth of Camille Claudel, Van Gogh... the damned artist, who lives in misery and does not enjoy any consecration until after her death. There is a well-rooted belief that alternative culture must be free. The majority of queer and female artists and directors are poor, precisely because they work without self-censorship, without producers, with little money or resources. The majority take jobs just to survive, or they are made redundant, and those who benefit from public or private money without having to worry about selling their art or paying their rent are rare. The production of a film is very expensive, and very often alternative artists cannot find producers to pay for everything.

The artists I spend time with help each other by working on each others' projects. We set the "system D" [coping strategies – trans.] in motion. It's a nice vibe but it's exhausting sometimes!

How does your work answer the concerns and criticisms of porn voiced by abolitionist feminists?

The sexophobic arguments of abolitionists create a great feeling of malaise in women and lesbians. The patriarchal system gives some crumbs of power to abolitionist feminists, since it gives power to people who erode freedoms by blaming women, disparaging some and valorizing others. There is nothing more dangerous for women's pleasure and freedom than a woman who passes moral judgment on another woman.

At the same time, family planning and abortion centers are closing down one after the other. Sexual education in schools boils down to being able to fit a condom on a banana after having been shown shocking videos of childbirth. They never mention pleasure. Abolitionist feminists play the game of the patriarchal system by imposing their puritanical morals on the rest of the women across the world. We can see their influence on social networks: before, you could still show bare breasts. Now, you cannot any longer. Even the image of a woman breastfeeding her child risks being censored. A video where one can catch a glimpse of a breast on YouTube or of girls kissing that does not correspond to heterosexual clichés about sexy lesbians (like those girls who have too much of a butch air!) and *bam!*, it's censored. The system of denouncement rules. For example, it is much more frequent for an LGBTQ image or video to be denounced than a sexist or racist image. LGBTQ artists, or those who work on the body, experience this pressure. Even world-celebrated paintings such as *The Origin of the World* by Courbet are censored!

All this becomes serious because little by little, insidiously, it changes our own vision of what is or is not shocking. Italy is a case in point, where an MP is trying to get gay kisses banned from TV before 10pm. It can go very far. In France, at the moment, this is true even of prostitution. Abolitionist feminists seek to promote a moralizing and illiberal bill, which has already proven dangerous for the security of women in other countries. Of course the criminal networks that exploit women and men against their will must be fought against. But it is not by making sexual labor illegal that one fights this kind of slavery. This law does nothing but make sexual labor more hidden, pushing it underground. Sex workers can't any longer practice their profession where they wish, they have to hide, at the risk of being arrested by the police. Thus, prostitutes do not have access to healthcare any longer and put their health in danger. Sex workers also have to work isolated, far from cities and safe places, and they become much more vulnerable to rapes, aggressions, blackmail, exploitation. In the name of puritanism and legality, society always seeks to lock women into a moralizing prison.

If the exploitation of sex in mainstream representations creates alienation and makes relationships between people more difficult, does feminist/queer porn provide an alternative for the creation of new subjectivities?

Perhaps our fantasies reflect an alienating system, and a first step purports to establish a difference between fantasy, sexual games (between consenting adults) and our behavior in society, in the family, in our daily relations. The difference must be established between the sexual game and reality, being conscious of power dynamics.

Feminist porn can also contribute a lot in terms of sexual education and of well-being for women. For example, I took part in a video, available on the Yagg website, concerning lesbian health. I also took part in the very first French campaign on health, sexuality and visibility for lesbians: "Comment ça va les filles? [How are you doing, girls?]." It's a participatory campaign of information, videos, chats and blogs on lesbian health, sexuality and visibility, in partnership with INPES (the National Institute for Health, Prevention and Education). The idea was to diffuse a positive and joyful message to launch the campaign. For that, they asked me to make a video on the prevention of STDs and the use of condoms on sex toys among lesbians. People could get informed thanks to the videos and the articles made available online: they could ask their questions to health and sexuality experts (for example about STIs, gynecological issues, the sourcing of different products, well-being in general), but also react on the forums, and more...

Open Letter on Empowerment and Queer Porn

Kathryn Fischer

There is nothing inherently empowering about making porn or showing the naked female (or any gendered) body on stage. The empowering part I believe, is primarily based in our freedom to explore what we are actually interested in, asking ourselves about life, and what we love to do. This could include, but is not limited to, discovering that we are exhibitionists or artists and/or that we enjoy exploring our sexuality with lots of different kinds of people. The freedom to explore these things – without feeling pressure from speculations about our gender or sexual orientation and without feeling shame about what we are publicly "allowed" to do or express out loud as those genders and orientations – deflates the imagined magnitude of what it is to show our bodies' sexuality in public.

If we are to speak of empowerment anyway – and to be honest I have a problem with the word because it recalls a top-down approach regarding teaching – I suggest we think of empowerment as personal and relative, and as a process. Who is anyone to say what is or is not empowering to any given person? What academic or researcher knows exactly what it means to be empowered when truly, speaking for myself, I am never fully empowered? It is an endless path that has no end. Empowerment must be a constant process that I (and only I) can understand for myself.

As an actress in queer porn and as a sexually explicit performer, I am certainly not arguing that an empowered woman has to make porn, be a publicly sexual creature or enjoy queer sex. Within some privileged circles it's been framed as fashionable to buy sex toys and learn how to use them, with the insinuation that a woman who doesn't isn't empowered. I disagree. For some this is empowerment and for others it is neither empowering nor disempowering, it is simply not relevant to their questions about life.

I think it's important that we (as studiers, as studied, or both) back away from trying to sound smart (not to mention binary) about the topic of porn in general – is it or is it not empowering, is it or is it not feminist – and ask really basic questions of each other, like: So, tell me, how did you feel when you were having sex on camera? Was it fun? Was it sexy? How are your clients these days? How was your day at work?

Thankfully, I have a community of queers around me who are willing and interested in engaging with me on these questions, people who talk about what we're creating these days on screen and how it feels. We've created a space where nuance is okay. It's alright to say: Everything about that porn set was designed to be safe and fun, but I still felt like the film maker wasn't fully prepared for what was going to happen and therefore I felt like I could have been better taken care of. It's important for me to have a community that is going to listen to me talk like that without feeling like I have to defend my interest in continuing to make porn.

Nevertheless, what makes the kind of porn I like to make different? What makes it queer? Why does our environment feel so good? The queer feminist porn set is a safe, circumscribed environment where everything that's consensual is okay. That's just one reason why I enjoy making it. Like a sex party, everyone is there to have sex (or watch), but unlike a sex party, I not only have permission to have sex, I actually have a prearranged agreement that I'll be taking part, always with the option to opt out. I don't have to guess or wonder whether someone is interested in having sex with me or whether or not I'm correctly understanding eye contact. Sometimes I get to have sex with someone that wouldn't ordinarily have sex with me or pick me out of a crowd (or vice versa). Sometimes in a party situation my identity gets interpreted on a quick, superficial level, whereas on a porn set I can assert or even role-play any identity that I define. For example, I can play a dominant butch even when I feel more like a switch. Or I can have sex with a butch who off-set might be attracted to more of a femme than I actually am. The porn set is an exciting way to make contact with a stranger or an acquaintance, and when the set is comprised of a closed community of people that I trust, the entire process of designing the scene, creating the scene, and filming can become something of an artistic, sexual, and spiritual orgy.

In the summer of 2009 I was honored to be part of the *Queer X Tour* (documented by Emilie Jouvet in the film *Too Much Pussy: Feminist Sluts in the Queer X Show*) – a group of queer activists, performers, sex workers, and pornographers that traveled through Europe performing a queer variety show about sex, porn, and gender. Along the way we made porn with each other and new friends that we picked up. The scenes were sometimes well planned out beforehand and at other times rather impromptu. The participants in each scene were always chosen with every participant's consent – a combination of deciding for ourselves who we were drawn to and letting the director (Emilie Jouvet) put together a combination that we could agree upon.

I personally like to be surprised; I find it fun and exciting to have sex with someone that I wouldn't necessarily be drawn to at first. I learn a lot that way, too. We were allowed to submit our own personal fantasies as ideas and either create a scene out of our own fantasy or agree to take part in another person's fantasy. For example, one person said, "I've always dreamed of a femme gangbang of three women on a switch." I've never personally had that fantasy and I don't even identify as femme, but something drew me into the role-play of it, dressing and playing the role of high femme coming into the house of a switch and fucking her. While I did know the other girls playing femme (girls on tour with me that I loved and trusted), I didn't know the person we'd be fucking beforehand and this is part of what drew me to the experience.

All of what I've described is part of what makes queer porn queer for me – the idea that choice, agency, consent, discovery, friendship, and love are present on the set. Also part of queer porn for me is the diversity of bodies, cultural, ethnic, and sexual orientations as well as varying combinations of body parts and toys coming together to bring real pleasure to another person, who can but doesn't have to express that pleasure through orgasm or a "cum shot." For me, queer porn is not about which body parts are represented on screen. Just because two people are similarly sexed (which is at best an approximation anyway because of the spectrum of genitalia we have and represent) does not mean that they are similarly gendered, so every encounter between two persons is an encounter of people who are not exactly what I would call "homosexual." Therefore I personally don't define queer porn by the words "similarly sexed" at all.

As I've explored what it means to subvert archetypes through my many mediums – performance artist, dancer, and porn actress – for me the queerness of queer porn is not on the surface, i.e., in what the sex looks like. It has much more to do with the intention with which we make porn together. Our intention is the way that we approach the project which can include all of the following and more: creating a safer-sex environment in which we are free to explore without fearing to contract STIs or bacterial infections, where the food for the set is cooked with love and consciousness about where it came from, and where decisions about the scene itself as well as the day's shooting plan are made in a non-hierarchical way. On a queer porn set, political themes and themes relevant to our community as queers are all welcome – a porn film, for example, can both be hot and explore the difficulties of watching a partner transition from female to male or the struggles of sharing a lover with another person. A queer porn set is a place where our intention to be inclusive and feminist is inherent in our approach. In the end, the intention will show its face on the screen and in the hotness of the sex. I have complete confidence that the audience will feel the intention in ways that we can't entirely predict.

Like any project taken up by like-minded and well-intentioned persons, however, queer porn is not always as liberating as it could be. But that doesn't mean I'm going to stop engaging with it or that I'm going to stop saying: it's political and it is also fun.

As much as it's important to take seriously both ourselves as feminists and our struggles as queers, it's also really important that we are allowed to take ourselves not so seriously. I like to have a joke and say, "Don't worry, I'm not working in that evil exploitative mainstream porn industry – I only work with DIY queer productions that can't afford to pay me anything." That's my kind of humor. And I mean it. It's true that all the porn I've ever made has always been for free because I love to be part of a queer, feminist, low-budget, DIY porn movement. But seriously, I would like to quit my waitress job. I'd like to never work as a burlesque dancer for Jaegermeister ever again. It's sometimes hard for others to understand what it really means not to have a financial safety net and the ways that work/sex/art/choice are intertwined in complicated ways.

Queer porn and the making of porn by self-proclaimed feminists will probably never go uncontested. But one thing it can't help being is a documentation of a movement of queers who at least believe for themselves that they are doing the right thing, that they are having fun doing it, and that this is how they like to have sex. There is a lot of material just in that alone that will speak for generations about how today's queer feminist community has sex and what kinds of themes they are dealing with in their sexual lives. I for one count myself lucky to be part of it.

This year I shared the experience of watching *Too Much Pussy* in a public screening in San Francisco with my mother, who is straight and could be called a second-wave, "anti-porn" feminist. Yet she stood by me. What an honor and what a true testament to that which is radical. Because at heart what is really queer, really revolutionary, and really powerful, is working at relationships with each other, receiving each other with love, understanding each other, trying to find out about each other, making assumptions for the best, and supporting each other on good and bad days.

A Seductive Intrigue of Sexuality?

Sinan Goknur

While most critiques of – as well as support for – explicit sexuality are framed in terms of morality, exploitation, and misogyny vs. empowerment, agency and sexual liberation, Baudrillard's polemical twist invites us to reconsider the matter from a different angle. In his article "Dust Breeding," he frames explicit sexuality (e.g., live sex events, porn, etc.) as yet another manifestation of our collective urge to demystify life into a banal reality.[1] He disregards the possibility of liberation through acts that hasten sexuality into integral reality, when the very essence of power lies in ascribing to reality everything that was in the order of dreams. By integral reality, Baudrillard refers to the procedure, which is accelerated by modernity, whereby everything becomes real, visible, transparent, "liberated," and legible to cultural and political regimes and whereby there is no longer anything on which there is nothing to say. He argues that sexuality is at best a hypothesis, and that as a hypothesis it does not make sense to strive for a systematic "liberation" through affirming the act. Rather, he contends that explicitness merely causes sexuality to lose its authority and its aura, the essential qualities that it once took on through repression.

---

1   Jean Baudrillard, "Dust Breeding," in Jean Baudrillard and Sylvère Lotringer (eds), *The Conspiracy of Art: Manifestos, Interviews, Essays* (New York: Semiotext(e), 2005), 181–88. Baudrillard makes a similar argument earlier in *Seduction* (New York: St. Martin's Press, 1991).

If Baudrillard is right, in our efforts to liberate sexuality from the grip of morality we face the danger of turning our desires and imagination into explicit and assimilable bits and pieces. But his attribution of sexuality's appeal to repression – hence the implied romanticization of that which we have only known in patriarchal terms – seems narrow-mindedly heterosexual and male-centric. If the issue is the loss of sexuality's enigma, why should we endorse repression, which ascribes sexuality to the hegemonic moral order and as such depletes its liveliness that exceeds the procedures of meaning making? After all, a regime of control frames its object of repression. Under patriarchal repression, the sexuality that Baudrillard romanticizes is made to come down from the order of dreams and land in the terrain of heterosexist imagination and male-centric desire. If graphic sexuality is banal because it conforms to the regime of visuality, then repressed sexuality is not any less banal, for it conforms to yet another hegemonic order: the regime of patriarchy.

On the other hand, when Baudrillard's patriarchal nostalgia is left aside, his argument opens up a stimulating question: If sexuality cannot be proven by means of sex and if merely affirming the act becomes trivializing after a while, what kinds of hypotheses on sexuality may cultivate its subversive edge? But before I go further, here is a self-disclosure that will clarify my personal investment in this somewhat pedantic quest for the meaning of sexuality and its implications for sexuality politics: I am a transgender person and sexuality has been an enigmatic lifesaver for me. Through queer sexuality, I got to experience multi-layered, sensual, sensorial, physical, spiritual, and imaginative bodily connections with other human beings, and these connections allowed me to comprehend my body with all of its conflicting complexities and dreaminess that are denied by the integral reality and its social and scientific categorizations. I think sexuality is revolutionary because it has the capacity to defy established claims and assumptions made about human physicality, drives, and desires. It is a realm in which bodies can weave in and out of social, sensorial, surreal, corporeal, and metaphysical fields that are usually not traversed in one go. If I had to think of something akin to my adult experience of sexuality, I would probably cite a quality from early childhood, the so-called inability to distinguish where physical reality stops and dreams begin – or the ability to weave these together, depending on how you look at it. A kindred domain would be art.

When I first started getting involved in queer and feminist sexuality politics in my early 20s, although I did find the enigma of sexuality vital to its emancipatory capacity, I thought of enigma as counterproductive to politics and an obstacle in the way of demystification and breaking of taboos. The political discourses that I became familiar with mostly saw sexuality as both a victim of power and an opposition to it. So queer and feminist sexuality for me meant resistance and transgression. But as such, rebellious and revolutionary visions of sexuality became contingent on its main oppressor, namely patriarchy. We advocated for visibility because patriarchal morality repressed and shamed sexuality; we wanted sexuality to be in the open because we thought its taboo status enabled easier patriarchal manipulation; we reclaimed sexual pleasure because it was largely denied to women and queer people. These issues are still valid and will maintain their urgency as long as patriarchal monopoly rules over sexuality and its twisted morality continues to choke it. On the other hand, in the past decade or so, some things changed, and I started to wonder about other directions we could take.

As recently as a decade ago, queer porn was not really available, and among the feminist groups I participated in, the notion of sexuality was mostly discussed within the context of sexual violence and trauma. But since then, the tides have turned, queer and feminist colleagues organize porn screenings and workshops, sexuality and sexual pleasure is more commonly embraced as a form of empowerment, and queer porn has become prolific and more accessible. It is starting to become an industry (hopefully without exploitative practices common in heterosexual porn industry). At the same time, our generation witnessed the bittersweet transformation of queer cultural productions from going unrecognized and being rejected toward being appropriated and commodified. The appropriation happened particularly to things produced within hegemonic paradigms, even when their queered contents initially presented a challenge. For instance in pornography, even though queer porn challenges the central position of heterosexual male desire, it still follows similar pornographic formats that prioritize the visual for the translation of sexual experience and as such remains susceptible to Baudrillard's critique. So I ask myself, in our efforts to rebel against the patriarchal and heterosexist sexual order, are we still conforming to its forms and as such contributing to its processes of trivialization of an undeniably seductive and subversive force in life?

My position is not to let go of the efforts for visibility of queer and feminist sexual practices by any means, because they still disrupt patriarchal control over sexuality, and so are necessary. Rather, I am intrigued by the political possibilities that may open up when we consider the angle of trivialization and delve into the concept of sexuality, which is about as elusive as a concept can get. Intersectionality is already an important part of that inquiry for it calls for an interrelated understanding of systems of oppression and for the examination of sexuality in relation to other social, biological, and cultural categories. Does Baudrillard's microscopic push – which contrasts with the telescopic inquiry of intersectionality – add any value to this discussion? I think so. The booming regime of vision and visibility, not only in the military–security domain but also in the domains of health and daily life via things like sensor data driven biomedical technology and personal gadgets, is infringing on aspects of our bodies that we never considered to be visible before. If we understand sexuality under these circumstances as the vehicle and effect of power, we also need to contend with power's subsumption (and our ascription) of all phenomena of life into integral reality, in which they become readily available as targets to destroy, as capabilities to exploit, as commodities from which to make profit, etc.

In the face of all this, what can we do? Perhaps Baudrillard would recommend disappearance. But I am not such a nihilist. I think the more useful concept that he offers us is seduction, which he defines as something not placed in sex or desire but in the play between sex and desire. Perhaps the notion of seduction can help us stay grounded in an enigmatic sense of sexuality while navigating our way in the maze of patriarchal oppression and control. In the end, even if the path to emancipation entails demystification, blowing off the smoke does not necessarily lead us out of the mirrors. So perhaps we can continue dreaming of a sense of sexuality that exceeds all that can be uttered about it, something inclusive of but not limited to sex, something that connects us back to the basics, these strangely shaped lumps of matter, full of senses, intact yet transient, our bodies as the rhythm keepers of all passions, our passions wild like the sea, along with the intuition that says, even under the sinister grip of control and integral reality, sexuality connects us to our vital seduction.

Everyday Porn

Namita Aavriti

In a channel for amateur pornographic videos online, an odd video bobs into view titled "Crowded Bus." This video has about 6,900,000 hits. A person sitting in the front section of a bus has shot this video, and its lingering, intrusive gaze passes over various women seated and standing around. One or two of them notice the camera and give irritated glances. Most ignore it and continue talking or staring into the distance, the banality of their daily commute undisturbed by this almost idiotic and perverse sexual gaze on bodies packed into a bus. Buses and trains are spaces in India where women are often harassed; hence the separation of the bus into gendered zones so that women can sit safely in the front. But these are also spaces in which myriad consensual yet covert sexual encounters are taking place between people.

The camera in this video could almost be a prosthetic extension, acting like a hand passing over the different bodies. Yet it is also the presence of the camera as a technological device and its ability to capture from within and yet separated from the encounter, that sexualizes this moment – a moment in which, technically speaking, nothing overtly erotic takes place. Perhaps the pornographic in this video also is in encountering the video in a collection of other far more obviously sexual videos. The viewer is possibly encased in a private space, whether watching on a mobile phone, in their room on a laptop or computer, or in the booth of a musty cyber cafe. The context of the encounter with the video, whether private or not, is another point at which the ordinary becomes sexualized, and the bodies of women caught in the routines of their daily life become available as video pornography.

Pornography is a genre of visual material that is defined by certain characteristics that have become fixed and even predictable with time. Pornography is sexually explicit and has semi or total nudity. Amateur pornography in India may often escape or defy the characteristics of the genre. In one video that is described as *kaand* (which could loosely translate as scandal or scandalous), the man behind the camera is heard serenading a woman with an old film song, and she looks coyly into the camera as she loosens her clothes at the end of her day, removes her shoes and rubs her feet. The video ends with an embrace between them, as the camera is turned to capture them both. These almost romantic or subtly erotic videos are definitely the exceptions in the stream of fairly obviously sexual videos. They also could be stubs that refer to more sexual videos. The genre of conventional or Western pornography has evolved a fixed rhythm and pattern that mimics or caters to human arousal and climax, and it must include specific sexual acts like blowjobs and penetration to be recognizable as pornography. In the context of amateur pornography in India, these 'markers' of course could be present in the video clips, but often are not. This could be because of the clandestine or hurried way in which such videos are shot. The clips capture a moment that is not staged — sometimes a person switches off the camera between sexual acts as if to mark a moment when the camera must now exit. Often clips are 10 seconds to a minute long and are just glimpses into a sexual act.

While some videos are leaked images of celebrities or public figures such as godmen or gurus, politicians, actors, but an overwhelming number of these amateur porn videos show ordinary lives and people. These are shot on low-resolution cameras, and the grainy texture of these videos is speckled with the hazy suggestion of bodies and body parts.

Porno-Tactics

The beginnings of amateur video porn in India can be traced back to 2001, when a private video of a couple was leaked into public circulation (Mysore Mallige). In 2004, a boy (school student in Delhi) made a MMS clip that suggested a blowjob, and this also got leaked. Since the early 2000s and advent of various digital technologies of image making and distribution, there has been a thriving network of the exchange and production of amateur porn, between local search engines, torrent services and piracy markets – exactly the same apparatus that makes citizen journalism, autonomous archives and independent online video possible. Amateur video porn is thus a distinct product of a wider contemporary and digital turn. It is made using cheap digital equipment, ranging from the mobile phone camera to handheld digital cameras. Online and offline networks of distribution allow for circulation that avoids the state's attempts to strictly govern media circulation. Can this mode of circulation, production and distribution that is independent, outside of State control and tactical in its use of available technology, of people and of other resources, be described as a sort of porno-tactics?

Pornography is a blind spot for the Indian State. Since independence in 1947, the courts in India have adjudicated on the matter of obscenity – this has included short stories, scenes in movies that are suggestive but not explicit, nudity in paintings and art. Thus there are stringent standards of obscenity for what circulates in the mainstream (newspapers, television, cinema etc.), even while a robust circulation of semi-pornographic and salacious books, magazines and soft porn films continue to thrive. Pornography as a specific category is not mentioned in Indian law, except under recent amendments to the Information Technology Act, 2000. Paradoxically obscenity is the legal category within which pornography is subsumed and also left out.

Recent decisions of the courts sensibly alter parameters of what can be called obscene to suit contemporary standards and that the courts must judge the work as a whole, whether it is a painting, art, film or book, rather than only parts of it. For instance, in a recent judgment about a painting by the famous artist, M.F. Hussain, it was argued that nudity per se is not enough for a work to be declared obscene because in certain forms of art, nudity conveys meanings other than the sexual which must also be taken into consideration by the court.

The Scandal of Nether Networks

In the incident regarding school students and the circulation of a MMS clip mentioned before, there was also an attempt to sell this MMS clip for approximately 2 dollars. The clip contained conversations between the boy and the girl that suggested sexual activity and minimal nudity (only the girl is visible in the clip). A college student (not connected to the school students) attempted to sell the video clip on a website called Bazee, which was then a subsidiary of eBay. A case was filed against the CEO of the website. The judgment laid down preliminary standards, which gave a very high level of responsibility to intermediaries i.e. those who provide the space onto which others can upload content. All those who provided open spaces online such as webzines, bulletin boards, hosting services and so on, were swept under this umbrella term of intermediaries who could be held responsible for content uploaded by others. This effectively ensured a high degree of control over how the internet was used and concomitantly authorized the shrinking of public spaces for free speech and discussion outside the purview of the State. Later these standards for intermediaries were passed as an amendment to the IT Act.

The legal response to the MMS incident should have focussed on the violation of privacy and trust of the girl captured in the video. In 2012, when a girl was gang raped and murdered in Delhi, a slew of legal reforms took place that altered sexual assault law and it was in these changes that finally there was specific recognition of the offence of taking or circulating a video without the consent of the people whose image has been captured.

But till these legal reforms in 2013, the legal response to the scandal of the circulation of this particular MMS clip involving school students and all other kinds of pornographic material has ultimately provided the state with new mechanisms to control speech through website managers, internet service providers, social media services and the companies that provide them. The state's anxiety about free speech is not so much about the content of the material or the images in them, as about the networks through which it can be disseminated. This is most evident in such legal responses to the illicit circulation of pirated and pornographic material, which includes the occasional banning of mobile phones in schools, shut down or restrictions on messaging services, raids on piracy stores, detailed regulations for cyber-cafes and so on.

While the state attempts to fix responsibility and liability, the circulation of a slippery object like a short MMS clip on the internet makes it difficult, to fix blame for transactions, for they keep extending and transferring through nodes in the network. These could be described as porno-tactics – the anonymity and multitude that characterizes covert consumption of pornography and the tacit agreements that allow for mass circulation to take place, away from the public eye and legal gaze.

Someone Like You

At a cheap Chinese restaurant, a friend of mine leaned across the dirty white tablecloth and in a hushed, urgent voice said - "That really young girl at the next table, I think I've seen her in a porn video." There is something amusing and uncanny about this moment. The pixelated nature of mobile phone porn makes it hard to fix on a person in a porn clip, for they are simultaneously nobody you will ever know and everyone you will ever meet. In the Indian context the images are often grainy because cheap mobile phone cameras are used for recording, and often people in these videos deliberately turn their faces away or keep it an angle so only certain rather obvious features like skin or hair color and slight details of the face are apparent. Identity is cloaked and if inadvertently, identity is leaked, then these videos ferociously circulate as scandal and porn.

Scandal is actually used as a category of Indian pornography – a specific entry in the lexicon of online pornography that usually lists categories in terms of acts or bodies (such as threesomes, multi-racial, Asian, gay, anal). Scandal and *kaand*, as it is sometimes colloquially referred to, is a specific kind of video where it is likely the girl is either unaware of the existence of the camera or trusts her lover with it. Some of these videos are no bigger than 200 pixels in resolution and the hidden, stationary camera barely captures the conversations or "action." It is the knife-edge of duplicity that makes these videos compelling.

Often video porn reveals the nastiness of gender, caste and class related dichotomies in direct and personal ways. A young girl is forced to reveal her name during a blowjob, another has her *kurta* (shirt) pulled off too abruptly, rapes are recorded and shared, vulnerable girls from lower castes are targeted and their images and bodies are trafficked. The vast majority of the everyday pornographic reflects and reveals how the configurations of caste and patriarchy are enacted on the body of a woman, particularly one who might be in need of livelihood or money.

A few video clips accidentally escape these configurations – a man struggles to keep a hard-on for a bored woman, who flings her hair over her shoulder in a gesture of feminine superiority and disdain at this profoundly ordinary moment. In Mysore Mallige, the gaze of the camera lingers on the girl's body before and after she bathes, while she changes clothes or just walks around the room. Her naked body and her longing gaze are both centerpieces for the camera that shoots everything in night shot mode, giving it a greenish tint that simultaneously renders it ghostly, amateur and intimate.

These gritty videos are the under tow of illicit media circulation, and can be summoned from the darker, intestinal cavities of the internet with keywords such as <scandal> <desi sex> <kaand> <hostel> <porn> <naked> <nude> <savita bhabhi> <hot aunty> <hot pictures> <nityananda> <tiwari> <sting> <sex tape> <dps mms> <debonair> <hidden camera> <changing room> <human digest> <surveillance camera> <web cam sex> <cyber café sex> etc. These videos cannot make any claim to radical politics around gender, sexuality and ethics, and like most pornography they work for heteronormativity rather than to destabilize it. Amateur pornography pose troubling questions about ethics, trust and the power relations within which they are made, but legal questions about consent and privacy are rarely raised in public discourse, while those regarding culture and women's roles are. Several videos that form part of these subterranean pornographic video cultures are of harassment, even rape or other kinds of sexual assault, Pornotactics are that which allow even such invasive and unethical material to evade the stranglehold of law and technology on circulation

Pornography is popularly considered to be the easy response to desire and frustration – it is simply about masturbation and sexual pleasure, and unlike cinema it doesn't complicate with narrative and subjectivity. It could be staged or performed and as a genre it is about depicting and evincing real corporeal pleasure (arousal and climax). Amateur pornography is also ostensibly about the same – about giving pleasure by capturing the real. But it also cannot evade the real and carries with it the divisions of the society and its most entrenched hierarchies. While watching we feel we know these people who are seemingly like us, and so we are caught between the cinematic pull of these images and the corporeal pull of pornography and arousal. It is reality television, it is intimate and it is often a betrayal of someone's trust, someone just like you and even sometimes a horrific violation. Amateur video, in contrast to large-screen cinema, is on a small or miniature screen that feeds into and off desire and fear. It is a parasitic or symbiotic beast that exchanges and sucks (bandwidth usage for pleasure, money for gratification), leaving a trail of dread and fascination about the "realness" of its uncanny images.

Look! But Also, Touch!: Theorizing Images of Trans Eroticism Beyond a Politics of Visual Essentialism

Eliza Steinbock

Introducing Public Confessions: "Wringing the Turkey's Neck"

Jamison Green's essay "Look! No, Don't!: The Visibility Dilemma for Transsexual Men" discusses the conflict between on the one hand claiming that "we" transsexuals want to be invisible, while on the other hand begging to be acknowledged. The activism that demands that society "Look!" is carried out through what Green calls "public 'confessions,'" revelations that are situated beyond family, lovers, and doctors in increasingly public spaces such as classrooms, the television, and especially, in films.[1] The counter-imperative "No, don't!," as Green explains, relates to being caught up in the regulation of transsexual treatment, in which "in order to be a good – or successful – transsexual person, one is not supposed to be a transsexual person at all."[2] At least from a medical perspective, the aim of hormonal and surgical treatment is to make the patient feel "normal" (that is, non-transsexual or dysphoric), a cure embodied by not drawing attention to oneself as transsexual.

---

1   Jamison Green, "Look! No, Don't!: The Visibility Dilemma for Transsexual Men," in S. Whittle and K. More (eds), *Reclaiming Genders: Transsexual Grammars at the* fin de siècle (London: Cassell, 1999), 117–31, at 118.
2   Ibid., 120.

The domain of sexuality functions as a key mode of achieving this disappearing act into normalcy. In the American Psychiatric Association's *Diagnostic and Statistical Manual of Mental Disorders: DSM IV*, which sets formal standards in psychology around the world, the diagnostic nomenclature of Gender Identity Disorder (formally Transsexualism) painstakingly excludes non-heterosexual and non-reproductive eroticism from this pathology.[3] Becoming positively diagnosed is the first step to (legally) accessing hormonal and surgical treatments in those countries that follow *The World Professional Association for Transgender Health* (WPATH) "Standards of Care" guidelines. If you find any element of your pre-transition embodiment sexually arousing or even enjoyable, then you might not actually desire the full range of treatments for genital reconstruction and thus not be a true transsexual. If you masturbate or have sex while "cross-dressed," then you could be a transvestite instead. Or, if your gender identity is the same as potential partners, and transitioning would produce gay or lesbian sexual identity, then the clinician might argue that the desire to transition comes from sexual identity confusion. Through the assumption of heterosexism, the hegemonic clinical discourse on gender dysphoria occludes a specified spectrum of trans(-)sexuality, a sexuality that follows from transitioning and non-binary genders.[4]

If for Green, the political struggle of trans self-representation produces a conflict expressed in the competing demands

---

3   American Psychiatric Association, *Diagnostic and Statistical Manual of Mental Disorders: DSM IV* (Arlington, VA: American Psychiatric Press, 1994).
4   For discussion in detail about the history of this nomenclature see Z. Davy, *Recognizing Transsexuals: Personal, Political and Medicolegal Embodiment* (Aldershot: Ashgate, 2011). In "'Sexing Up' Bodily Aesthetics: Notes towards Theorizing Trans Sexuality," in S. Hines and Y. Taylor (eds), *Sexualities: Past Reflections and Future Directions* (Basingstoke: Palgrave Macmillan, 2012), 266–85, Steinbock and Davy analyze the history of sexological and clinical parsing of transsexualism in terms of sexuality. The most recent controversial development in trans-focused sexology is known as the "Bailey Affair" (Burns, 2004). Here trans sexuality is once again purported to be a pathological expression of hypersexuality. In *The Man who would be Queen*, Bailey (2003), stresses the hypersexualization of two sub-types of male to female transsexuals, autogynephiles, and homosexual transsexuals.

of, "Look!" and "No, don't!," then alternatively, Sandy Stone's ground-breaking essay of 1991, "The 'Empire' Strikes Back: A Posttranssexual Manifesto," calls for the transsexual community to "Look!" at themselves. Or, to be more precise, for (post)transsexuals to be honest about their authentic desiring selves, and to show within their self-theorization of trans experience wider "spectra of desire."[5] It is crucial that the spectra be inclusive of trans desires that articulate trans sexual dissonances, those elements that would potentially exclude you from being diagnosed with transsexualism in the first place. The manifesto draws attention to a sexual spectrum in the trans archive, one that Stone suggests has been enjoyed covertly because of the repercussions that could be suffered if these dissonances were exposed.

Blowing the cover, Stone writes about an erotic act euphemistically called, "'wringing the turkey's neck', the ritual of penile masturbation just before surgery," which she claims is the most "secret of secret traditions."[6] One may consider that for potential and actual female-to-male transsexuals (FTMs, or transmen, or transmasculine transgender-identified people), such covert sexuality may include enjoyment of ("vaginal" or "front hole") penetration or other play involving "womanly" parts. Pre, post, non-op, or simply transgender embodied sexuality experienced by trans folk continues to be circumscribed by what Stone calls a "permissible range,"[7] a range which maps onto the same heterosexual matrix that delimits queer sex, kinky sex, and other deviations from the hetero norm. Under investigation in Stone's exposure of dissonant trans eroticism is the regulatory means of delimiting transsexualism as a normative gender and sexual condition.

Rather than restricting ourselves to the sense of sight embedded in the metaphor of *spectrum* of desire, one might also *feel* trans eroticism, as Susan Stryker describes it, as a *poiēsis* of the trans body, an aesthetic experience of oneself as "iridescent, shimmer-

---

5   S. Stone, "The 'Empire' Strikes Back: A Posttranssexual Manifesto [1991]," in S. Whittle and S. Stryker (eds) *The Transgender Studies Reader* (New York: Routledge, 2006), 221–35, at 231.
6   Ibid., 228.
7   Ibid.

ing," and, as these visual metaphors of movement suggest, also "unceasingly active in its inversions."[8] That is, one feels desire's shimmering activity through the synesthetic modalities of touch intertwining with vision. Taking Stone's example of "wringing the turkey's neck," the metaphor of strangulation, of "wringing" a neck, points to the key role of touch by the hand and on a body.

Isolating this moment of resistance to the permissible range of touch, the defiant touching of oneself and others perhaps also "wrings out" or takes control of the regulatory discourse. Following Stone's suggestion to look at instances of trans sexual dissonance, I argue for special attention to be paid to the ways in which the conflicting imperatives of "Look! No, don't!" are negotiated in public confessions of trans sexualities. Within trans pornography, where genitals are often on display, or at least the exposure of them is negotiated, we can examine the complicated political demand to look at this public confession of trans embodiment, but also the sexual invitation to touch it. Trans pornography may cite the identity politics of visibility, but it also offers a rich opportunity for investigating the force, shape, and experience of trans eroticism through touch.

Visual Essentialism: "Look!"

Pornography's conventions are often attuned to *realism* through showing bodies in close range that are caught up in sexual acts and hence, engaging viewers in the scopophilic richness of real bodies having apparently real sex. In the first instance, trans porn says, "Look! Trans sex is like this." The visual availability of the image contributes to the force of this imperative to "Look!" As Mieke Bal notes, an audience tends to go along with the general epistemological meaning of images on display – precisely by inviting the look to linger, they are invited to believe their transparent verac-

---

8 Susan Stryker, "Dungeon Intimacies: The Poetics of Transsexual Sadomasochism," *Parallax* 14, no. 1 (2008): 36–47.

ity, and to enjoy it.⁹ Within the genres of queer, trans, and other minority porn, the political wish to represent these marginalized sexual identities can lead to a conflation of political visibility with actual visible representation in pornographic images. The investment in the apparent empirical knowledge of "real" trans sexualities represented in trans porn has a history in waves of feminist revisionings of female and lesbian sexuality in the 1980s and 1990s. This history also struggled with what I call "visual essentialism," or, the mobilization of a mimetic medium and a genre with a history of scientism to represent identities of desire. The essentialism of the image appears to carry over into the essentialism of the identity represented therein.

One of the most influential theories of pornography's realist drive comes from Linda Williams, who uses the industry term "hard core" that reflects the investment in film to reveal an actual, real core. In *Hard Core: Power, Pleasure and the "Frenzy of the Visible,"* she historicizes pornography's origin and function through tracing Foucault's concept of *scientia sexualis* into more contemporary pornographies. Her thesis is that, in its "positivist quest for the truth of visible phenomena," as she characterizes pornography's endeavor, it turns out to be merely a masculinist measure of veracity.¹⁰ Whereas the penis's ability to provide evidence of pleasure through ejaculation is well aligned with positivism's preference for direct observation, women's pleasure ironically happens in an "invisible place."¹¹ This place is literally the black hole of the vagina. Given (her assumption) that women's orgasmic pleasure cannot be scientifically verified by external ejaculation, or other outward displays of sexual pleasure, it fails to measure up to the masculinist quest for empirical verification, thereby rendering it invisible and a problem that pornography tries both to solve, and to avoid, in its eternal return to the fetish of the "money shot."

---

9   Mieke Bal, *Double Exposures: The Subject of Cultural Analysis* (New York: Routledge, 1996), 8. This thesis is further developed in her article "Visual Essentialism and the Object of Culture," *Journal of Visual Culture* 2, no. 1 (2003), 5–32.
10 Linda Williams, *Hard Core: Power, Pleasure, and the "Frenzy of the Visible"* (Berkeley: California University Press, 1999 [1991]).
11 Ibid.

For Williams, women's, and, by extension, lesbians', sexuality remains in the closet and thus un-confessed; that is, female pleasure and sexual identity are invisible in the political realm of sexual representation. However, understanding porn in this way confuses capturing the "real" of the pro-filmic event with the capture of the "truth" of the actor's desire – thus with that desire's confession. Hence, Williams falls into the same trap of the phallocentric investment in visuality that she wishes to dispute. The doubled notion of visibility at work in her analysis of pornography mistakes the capture of acts and pleasures with the true confession of the individual's sexuality and desire. That this conflation of the cinematic privilege of realism with discursive truth has only recently been addressed[12] perhaps reflects the desire on the part of porn studies scholarship to establish itself as the study of a cultural discourse with a direct relation to political "realities," as Williams frames her study in the introduction.

Film theorist Ingrid Ryberg sees that Williams's harnessing of realist cinematic ontology to a sexual epistemology has contributed to a number of mixed visibility strategies in contemporary queer porn culture, such as obeying the principal of "maximum visibility" of the body, giving context to the performers' sex in a sexual community, and including confessional interviews in which the talents explain themselves.[13] All these visibility strategies are used in trans porn too, particularly in the stream of docu-porn from *Linda/Les and Annie: The First F-t-M Transsexual Love Story* (1989), to *Enough Man* (2005), to *Trans Entities: The Nasty Love of Papi and Wil* (2007) and the recent *Doing it Ourselves: The Trans Women Porn Project* (2010), as well as in the regular inclusion of transmasculinity (less so transfeminine talent) in marketed queer porn, such as *The Crash Pad Series* (2005–2012), *Speakeasy* (2010), and *Pornograflics* (2004). In her conclusion, Ryberg warns of the risk in assuming that by deploying explicit cinematic language to

---

12 Cf. C. Taylor, "Pornographic Confessions?: *Sex Work and Scientia Sexualis in Foucault and Linda Williams.*" Foucault Studies 7 (2009), 18–44.
13 Ingrid Ryberg, "Maximizing Visibility," *Film International* 6, no. 6 (2008), 72–79, at 72–74.

reveal all the body's sexual secrets one might then make visible marginalized subject positions and experiences. It is this mistaken conflation of political and representational "visibility," with its double investment in visual essentialism, that I wish to critique in the creation and reception of trans porn. While the moment of saying "Look!" is important to the political call for recognition, porn may also have political force on the bodily level of the viewer and for the performer. Hence, trans porn is political not simply because it reflects "real" bodies, desires, and experiences, but because it engenders them on and off the screen.

Aesthetic Experience: "Touch!"

The first step toward accounting for the politics of touch in trans porn involves recognizing the impact of embracing trans sexuality in general – in defiance of medical discourse that either de-eroticizes or hyper-eroticizes transsexualism. The erotic touching between trans porn talent on-screen and trans porn viewers off-screen may challenge the medical terms of transsexuality that have delimited eroticism for trans persons to heteronormative penetration and to the desire to transition itself. Secondly, regarding the politics of touch in trans porn, it is often overlooked how visual representations of sexually explicit acts also facilitate a haptically erotic experience. The everyday vernacular related to porn, which includes phrases like "one-handed reading" and "whatever turns your crank," suggests that at the base of pornography lies a synesthetic relationship of vision to touch similar to trans eroticism's shimmering *poiēsis*. Thus although it may suggest a mimetic relationship to reality, clearly porn also functions as an inter-subjective social space to explore and produce our sexual bodies. A good example of this call to both "Look!" and "Touch!" – this tension between the politics of visibility and the trans erotics of touch – is Barbara DeGenevieve's *Out of the Woods* (2002), in which both imperatives compete for attention from the viewer.

This short video was one of many scenes that she shot with participants who responded to the call to appear on the now offline website ssspread.com, which features "hot femmes, studly butches

Figs. 1–14. *Out of the Woods* (2002), dir. Barbara DeGenevieve (USA), 7 min. – *Fig.* 1.

Fig. 2.

and lots of genderfuck" (January 2001–February 2004).[14] Like the other scenes, DeGenevieve shot whatever the participants wanted. This format lends a sense of authenticity to the video, providing a kind of document of an unscripted and undirected sexual scene between transman JJ and transwoman Tennetty. The video's public display functions as a confession of their prior private experience of having sex, a "coming out of the [trans sexual] closet." A declaration that renders someone visible as a *sexual* transsexual, particularly a non-heteronormative transsexual, takes on acute political significance as it signals defiance of the range of permissible touch. Through both its production and its public circulation, *Out of the Woods* suggests that trans desire is "out" of the determining factors of psycho-sexual diagnosis: "out" of the "woods" that renders trans, in particular trans on trans, desire impossible and at the same time invisible. The emphatic "outness" in *Out of the Woods* signals the significance of eroticism to trans experience, which furthermore demands to be addressed as more than a deviant complication of male or female, and heterosexual or homosexual, subject positions.

The performative force of this trans sexual coming out, however, is rendered largely through the scene's use of physical and emotionally laden touch. Involving wrestling and powerplay, the performers never break contact after the first circling and taking down of each other (*figs.* 1 and 2). Bare-chested and barelegged, Tennetty's and JJ's skin very quickly becomes covered in the earth and pine needles that blanket the forest floor. Shots showing tousled and matted hair, dirt under nails, and impressed dead leaves on the body draw even more attention to their tactile experience. The vulnerability of their near nakedness (socks, shoes, and ripped fishnet tights stay on) is amplified by their flipping and slamming of one another into the ground (*figs.* 3, 4, and 5). While the handheld camera quietly tracks the progression of their sexual

---

14 This scene was made available personally through the director; however, DeGenevieve, who has now passed away, believed it would achieve commercial release through the production house Femme Fatale (Nan Kinney) on the compilation video *Rough Stuff: More Scenes from Ssspread.com*.

Fig. 3.

Fig. 4.

LOOK! BUT ALSO, TOUCH!

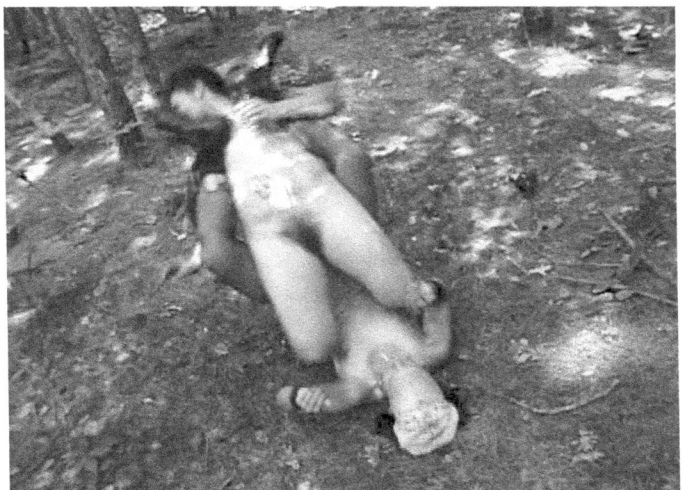

Fig. 5.

Fig. 6.

Fig. 7.

Fig. 8.

experience, moving to frame it from all sides in close-up and medium shots, Tennetty and JJ never glance into it. Absorbed in the intensity of the scene, the exchange of touches reverberates and amplifies through the alternation of caresses with slaps, punches, and grabs. Primarily, it is JJ, as a Top, or Dominant, who initiates contact, with Tennetty guiding, yielding, and encouraging the touches in movement and in sound (*figs.* 6 and 7).

With the careful application of a condom and lube, JJ prepares Tennetty for penetration, her back arching in sensual anticipation. As they begin to rollick and find a pleasurable rhythm, the camera comes closer to their bodies to focus on the pucker of skin, the concentration of pleasure on their faces (*fig.* 8). Noticeably, there is no "meat shot" or attempt to get between them to show us the penetration. Likewise, we have no access to a "money shot" to conclude the scene. Though no audible or visible orgasm is had, the intensity of the experience is felt in the capture of the aftercare.

The post-sex clean up would not normally be included in commercial porn formats. But here we drift seamlessly from the sex into the same attention to touch in the sensual closure of the scene. The white bandage that mysteriously had covered the front of Tennetty's crotch comes into focus. JJ backs her up towards a tree, gingerly guiding her exposed skin safely past the sharp edges of broken limbs sticking out akimbo from the tree's trunk (*fig.* 9). The so-called climax of the scene, in the place of a "money shot," is the very slow removal of Tennetty's bandage. At first seen from the side view, Tennetty lifts her leg over JJ's shoulder to allow him to reach the tape (*fig.* 10). Swinging to a frontal shot, JJ, now standing, starts to pull the tape off, a gesture that causes her skin to pull away from her body, eliciting a sensation of pain (*fig.* 11). Although painful now, the bandage's stickiness had provided a protective covering for her genitals, those that could not be directly touched by her sexual partner. She takes hold of the tender bits, gently massaging them (*fig.* 12) before relaxing into JJ's embrace (*fig.* 13), which concludes the scene.

The characters JJ as "Pants" and Tennetty as "Fishnets" (*fig.* 14) who appear on camera in "Out of the Woods" do not seek to

Fig. 9.

Fig. 10.

LOOK! BUT ALSO, TOUCH!

Fig. 11.

Fig. 12.

73

Fig. 13.

Out of the Woods

Pants.................JJ Bitch
Fishnets...........Tennetty

Fig. 14.

produce a documentation of their passing as cisgender, or to confess their chosen gender role. The talent bravely lets the camera into the space of their trans sexual practice, calling the audience to "Look!" at their shimmering spectrum of desire. In this way, *Out of the Woods* may be understood as part of Stone's summons for a "next transformation" within the community. This transformation is not linear. It seems to involve an alternative genealogy: rather than acceding to realness, it investigates gendered experience, it questions sexual authenticity and the ways we might conceive of trans sex through sensate understanding rather than through ocular determinism.

Nevertheless, *Out of the Woods* mobilizes its touching effects through the visual medium of digital video. In T*he Cinematic Body* (1993), Steven Shaviro singles out one quality of the image most responsible for filmic fascination: the image's appeal to tactility in combination with its simultaneous exclusion from touch. Shaviro describes it as follows, "I cannot take hold of it in return, but always find it shimmering just beyond my grasp."[15] This shimmering quality, which Stryker also attributes to trans embodiment, triggers a haptic response in the spectator: called to action, s/he lifts a hand, seeking to become caught up in the flux of images. As phenomenologist Vivian Sobchack theorizes through the film *The Piano,* barred from grasping the image, the viewer's hand recursively seeks out his or her own body at hand, to make sensate meaning of the image.[16] Perhaps even more literally, the viewer's grasp of their body while they look at pornography is a substitute for the body on-screen, a "one-handed" reading of the filmic text. *Out of the Woods* and other trans porn potentially depicts as well as generates a groping subject defying the permissible range of touch to engender trans erotics.

---

15 Steven Shaviro, *The Cinematic Body* (Minneapolis: Minnesota University Press, 1993), 47.
16 V. Sobchack, *Carnal Thoughts: Embodiment and Moving Image Culture* (Berkeley: California University Press, 2004), 76–78.

Pornography for Blind and Visually Impaired People: On Tactility and Monstrosity

Elia Charidi

In his novel *On Heroes and Tombs,* the Argentinean writer Ernesto Sabato incorporates artistically a series of beliefs and cultural obsessions that directly connect blindness to the concept of darkness – and to whatever that might entail. One of the novel's central figures, Fernando Vidal Olmos, attempts to bring to light the secrets of the Sect of the Blind, an organization which, in his deep-rooted belief, represents the Prince of Darkness and governs the world on his behalf in a shifty and infernal way and by using supernatural and invincible strengths. He thus begins a dangerous journey into the dark and underground world where he imagines the blind to initiate the new arrivals – that is, whoever has just lost their sight – and to plan their secret action. There, he finds himself in a boundless, deep and terrifying darkness, inhabited by serpents and snakes, bats and spiders, carnivorous birds that fly around him threatening him and eventually ripping out his eyes. In the tunnels he traverses looking for secret passages, the water stagnates and sticky creatures whose existence nobody could even imagine hide in the slime's dampness. Describing the chronicle of his research in "Report on the Blind," Fernando Vidal Olmos narrates:

> My thoughts had dwelt on this subterranean network [of the Buenos Aires draining-away system] more than once in my

> life, no doubt on account of my tendency to ponder such
> things as cellars, wells, tunnels, caves, caverns and everything
> that in one way or another is related to that enigmatic subter-
> ranean reality: lizards, snakes, rats, cockroaches, weasels and
> *the blind*.[1]

Lingering between illusion and reality and not knowing whether he actually lived what he narrates or had simply been subjected to the blind's magical powers, the hero sees them incarnated in a grotesque figure that belongs neither to human or animal kind. The blind are human, but sooner or later they will be transformed into snake- or bat-like creatures. Their lack of vision makes them beastly: they have damp palms, icy blood and sticky skin, abstract and vacant faces that stare severely, their senses of hearing and orientation are sharpened to a supernatural level. They are also characterized by intense mistrustfulness and maliciousness toward anyone that does not belong to their group. This rhetoric of the blind's bodily and spiritual monstrosity reaches its expressive culmination when the hero faces a blind, lascivious and perverted woman, who indulges in sexual orgies with countless lovers in front of her also blind and moreover paralyzed husband, in order to get revenge for the oppression and violence that he had exercised over her before he was disabled. For the needs of his unusual research, he follows her secretly and eventually engages in a series of sexual contacts with her. On this, he writes:

> I shall merely say that even if I were to live for five thousand
> years, it would be impossible for me to forget, to my dying
> day, those summer afternoon siestas with that nameless female
> as multiple as an octopus, as slow and minute as a slug, as
> flexible and perverse as a giant viper, as electric and hypnotic
> as a female cat in the night.[2]

---

[1] Ernesto Sabato, *On Heroes and Tombs* [1961], trans. Helen R. Lane (London: Jonathan Cape, 1990), 354. Emphasis added.
[2] Ibid., 345.

Sabato builds this close relationship between blindness and monstrosity on a series of multiple connected and deep-rooted cultural dualisms that relate to lack of vision. These include darkness vs. light, lie vs. truth, flesh vs. spirit, body vs. mind, subconscious vs. conscious, and meet their absolute expression in the figure of a female and sexually perverted monster, abandoned and led on by the desires of the flesh and the deeper, dark and uncontrolled instincts of hate and repulsion. Rather than the long-standing identification between femininity and body/flesh (in contrast to vision's intellectuality and its conceptualization as mainly a male attribute),[3] what interests here is that we find a variation of the relation between blindness and sexual monster in the first pornographic magazine created especially for blind and visually impaired people. Entitled *Tactile Minds,* it includes tactile pictures of naked women and men, all accompanied by descriptive texts in Braille. The goal of Canadian photographer and creator of the magazine, Lisa Murphy, was to fill a gap in the market: "There are no books of tactile pictures of nudes for adults. We're breaking new ground. *Playboy* has an edition with Braille wording, but there are no pictures," Murphy explains.[4]

Besides filling this commercial vacuum, the aim of the magazine was also to give blind people the opportunity to access the pornographic experience. Moved by her previous experience as a sighted volunteer at the Canadian National Institute for the Blind, Murphy realized that these people "have been left out in a culture saturated with sexual images." Her rhetoric is related to one of the main claims raised by the wider movement for the rights of people with disabilities regarding the relation between impairment and sexuality: they contend that the conversation needs to get out of the narrow private sphere and be published, at the same time de-

---

3 Indicatively, see J. Rose, *Sexuality in the Field of Vision* (London: Verso Books, 1986).
4 Lisa Murphy, *Tactile Minds* (2010). http://tactilemindbook.com. The initiative of including blind and visually impaired people in the industry of pornography belongs to Playboy magazine, when during 1970–1985 it converted in Braille the texts that accompanied the pictures. See also http://www.flashnews.com/news/wfn1100415fn8524.html

constructing the myth that people with disabilities have no sexual identity and desires.[5] Nevertheless, the issue in this article is not about whether this initiative can actually be a step towards the inclusion of blind people, but that it seems to give them access to a very particular kind of sexuality: that reflected in the figure of the "monster."

Murphy describes the process of creating the magazine. All of the bodies, featured in the magazine, which includes her own, belong to real persons, to women and men that volunteered to pose naked in front of the photographer's camera for the needs of the magazine. After that, and through a complex and lengthy procedure, every picture was converted into tactile image, using the same material as that used for printing Braille lettering.[6] Apart from some expected pornographic representations that correspond to current stereotypes of bodily beauty and aesthetics (the upper body of a woman with "perfect breasts" or of a muscular and fit man) and a mild kind of fetishism (including high-heeled shoes made of snake skin, earrings piercing erotic zones or objects that increase the size of the genitalia), what characterizes the collection's erotic atmosphere is the unusual representation of heads and faces. Everyone wears specially constructed bags or masks made of plastic, paper or cloth, in order to maintain their anonymity. As a result, not only faces but also bodies that deviate from the standards of human physiology are created. This is not only due to the covering itself, but also to particular choices over the aesthetics of the masks: heads in square, rectangular or perfect circles shapes, faces that look inexpressive, since they have no detailed characteristics, others in which the eyes or mouths are emphasized

---

5 Indicatively, see E.M. Murray and S.H. Jacobs, (2010). "Revealing Moments: Representations of Disability and Sexuality," in R. Sandell, J. Dodd & R. Garland-Thomson (eds), *Re-presenting Disability. Activism and Agency in the Museum* (London & New York: Routledge, 2010), 155–67.

6 The magazine is a handmade thermoform book consisting of 17, 3-D tactile photographs on white thermoform plastic pages with the visual image and descriptive Braille accompaniment. It measures 11 × 11.5 inches and is approximately 6 inches wide. It is held together by a simple spiral binding which allows the convenience of reading each diagram on a flat surface or removing pages.

in several ways (eyes that look like eggs or have been replaced by paper cones, a deep fissure instead of a mouth). However, the figures that dominate the magazine's pages, intensifying the sense of the abnormal, are those of people wearing animal masks. There are a variety of naked pictures that depict human bodies with animal heads, such as sheep, rabbit, frog, and elephant.

Murphy's project has been characterized as erotic, high fetish, or even pornographic. She stresses, however, that pornography is exclusively about the act of sexual contact and in this sense her book is a "nudie book." Nevertheless, the bodies that she crafts are not depicted in an innocent and neutral condition of natural nakedness – if ever there can be such a thing. On the contrary, they give off an intense sexuality that is constructed primarily from the mixture between human and animal elements (or between human and machine as in the case of a man dressed as a robot) and secondly from the uncanny sense that is provoked by the distortions of the heads' natural shapes or of their facial characteristics. It is precisely this naked and "abnormal" body, designated especially for blind people, that makes an impression, creates awkwardness and ultimately brings to mind Michel's Foucault analysis on abnormality.[7]

"The monster is the major model of every little deviation [...] the principle of intelligibility of all the forms that circulate as the small change of abnormality," Foucault says.[8] In other words, the monster is one of the basic figures through which the modern concept of the abnormal and at the same time pathological individual was constructed. The "human monster" is that creature where we find "the mixture of two realms", the animal and the human – or even the mixture of two species, of two individuals, of two sexes, of life and death.[9] Breaking the laws of nature and society and calling into question the natural borders and categorizations, it constituted the legal and biological problem of the eighteenth cen-

---

7   Michel Foucault, *Abnormal: Lectures at the Collège de France, 1974–1975*. (London & New York: Verso, 2003).
8   Ibid., 56.
9   Ibid., 63.

tury. During the next century and through a complex process of combining these different apparatuses of knowledge and power (of the legal and the medical), the psychiatric domain adopts the figure of the monster in order to split it into many tiny and everyday abnormalities, formatting what Foucault names the "technology of anomaly." From then on, the monster meets not only with crime, as had happened before, but also with everyday sexuality. A sexual anomaly is hidden behind almost every deviation; it is its root and its cause. And the body, with its desires and passions, is gradually turned into an object of minute examination and surveillance. We could say then that, whereas in the fictional world of Sabato the beastly sexuality of the blind was identified with their anomalous nature and idiosyncrasy – they were themselves kinds of monsters – in the context of pornography, monstrosity seems to be detached from the individual and to be incorporated into the object of its sexual desire: the body, or better, the body that is going to be touched. In this framework, the sense of touch seems to be one of the body's sensory details where the deviation from visual ability is localized and the abnormality of blindness is constructed.

Introducing touch into pornography, which is a domain that has been constructed mainly around visual representations, has been seen as a paradox by some critics of the magazine. It gives us the chance, however, to see how the practice of touch is constructed in erotic contexts. Conceptualized as a substitute for sight, Murphy asserts that what cannot be seen, can now be touched, offering analogous satisfaction and joy. In order for this hurried, though common, theory on the direct substitution of the senses to be sustained, many things have to be neglected, such as the fact that many blind people have memories of past visual representations before losing their sight; or the access they gain to things and even to visual representations through listening to sounds, as well as other people's oral descriptions. These are memories and experiences that register and shape the experience of touch itself; in other words, they mediate the relation between the object and the body-that-touches-in-order-to-perceive. In this sense, they may call into question the directness that is attributed by our visual culture to touch as a means of perceiving the world.

This "natural" directness seems to play an important role in that the particular pornographic material constructs blind people's sexual imaginary and desire in terms of monstrosity. What is being touched, that is the object of pleasure, seems to be transformed by the gesture of touch itself and to be converted into the grotesque figure of a sexual monster that embodies human and at the same time animal characteristics. As if touch, in other words, pollutes with its directness the object that is being touched by transmitting to it some of the downgrading qualities that have been attributed to it in the contexts of Christianity and European enlightenment: of carnal pleasure and sin, of animality and the non-rational. These are qualities which are all reduced to the conceptualization of touch as a bodily sense and are contrasted to the supposed detached, rational, objective, and scientific gaze of vision.

Having said this, I do not mean to underestimate Murphy's innovatory project, but to raise a question about the normative strands it implies. The problem is not that it presents blind people as sexual monsters; besides, the issue is that they are almost totally excluded from the entire sphere of the erotic. The problem instead is that their sexual desires and behaviors are characterized by monstrosity. This is a shifting that makes us wonder whether this tactile pornography, however inclusionary and liberating it wants to be, leaves enough space for the blind people to express and shape their pornographic fantasies according to their own sexual preferences or eventually comes to reinforce the already existing norms carved upon the body and tactility. [10]

---

10 Regarding the ambivalent role of monster and the danger to re-enter the normative narrations that it tries to undermine, see A. Athanasiou, "Μεταξύ Τεράτων και Συμβάντων: Τεχνολογίες του Έμφυλου Σώματος, Αναπλαισιώσεις του Ανθρώπινου [Between Monsters and Events: Technologies of the Gendered Body, Reframings of the Human]," in Ζωή στο Όριο. Δοκίμια για το Σώμα, το Φύλο και τη Βιοπολιτική [*Life at the Limit: Essays on the Body, Gender, and Biopolitics*] (Athens: Εκκρεμές, 2007), 167–88.

A Note on Pornography and Violence

Mantas Kvedaravicius

Investigator Lazanov asked me to sign a document. When I refused he called in three officers who picked up Michailov from the floor and bent him over. One of the officers squeezed the boy's head between his legs, the other pulled down his trousers. "Michailov, you are going to tell the truth," said Lazanov. He took a police baton from a table, went to a cupboard and opened a little door. I saw a plastic can with black shoe wax on one of the shelves. Lazanov dipped a tip of the police baton into the wax. After that he approached Michailov from behind and shoved the baton into his ass. I saw that baton going into the hole for ten centimetres. The other officer was filming, Michailov was shouting loud.

Broom handles and stool legs, cheap- champagne and Coke bottles, plastic tubes with barbed wire and police batons are all shoved in people's anuses to produce confessions, to force them to own up to crimes that they never committed or even imagined. Those wielding the tools hope this will help get them a promotion or keep within the demands of statistics, and will also give them pleasure. In other words these are legal instruments for making of thieves, terrorists, murderers, extremists, bandits, hooligans, or any sort of delinquent required by local economies and global politics. Indeed the materiality and the names of the tools testify to this: police batons are manufactured in rubber factories in little Russian towns, and stamped with revealing abbreviations such as

PUS (*palka universal'naia spetsial'naia,* "special universal stick") with clear specifications — "PUS-1 Argument," "PUS-2 Argument B," "PUS-3 Siurpriz," "PUS-4 Kontakt" — language that specifies the violence inherent in these objects. Investigators' offices, temporary detention facilities, military bases, penal colonies, torture basements in police stations... These factories-of-law-cum-pleasure-playgrounds use the acronyms (ROVD, ORB, FSB, ORC, UBOP, RUBOP, OVD) that within local vernacular are substitutable and inextricable from the history of terror extending to the KGB and its affiliates.[1] A lot has come out of these spaces: photographs, cellphone videos, journalist reports, legal documents, testimonies, interviews, stories told, retold, imagined, more signatures, confessions, trial recordings, legal protocols... Some sort of scene is built up of raped, mutilated, and objectified bodies, which seems to make violence compatible with pornography.

Probably most of it is coming through media from Russia's peripheries, from the centers and outskirts of contemporary empires, assembling their anti-terrorist vocabularies and legal edicts to use violence far and wide. Yet this article is also a reflection on words spoken by those who have been in these cells. It is an ethnography of senses, based on time spent while thinking and seeing things in Grozny, Chechnya after war had just ended (no one is sure when wars end but politicians put this date around 2005) — when intimate violence was being used more often than bombing itself. Seeing people coming in and out of buildings that practice these principles, makes you think of the relation between violence and pornography with less distance to the body and politics in question. Nonetheless distance is as important as representation.

These dark little spaces pressing on us in fragments of texts, images, blocks of emotions, through international and local media, academic discourse, in both sensational and down-to-earth ways, give rise to even more questions. How do we deal with images of mutilated bodies, with the pain of infringement, with all

---

[1] KGB — *Komitet Gosudarstvennoi Bezopasnosti* (Committee for State Security). The main security service institution of the Soviet Union that was serving as intelligence agency and secret police.

the suffering and historicities that come with it, with the cultures that code it? How do we reimagine these events when our imaginations is already absorbed and figured by the aesthetic field of body politics? And how is the penetration of bodily surface and the control of its movement, the injection of power into a body, figured upon the gazer, the spectator who is made to watch in order to be intimidated (although of course whether they are watching or being watched is questionable)? Or upon one who expresses agony in image and sound in order to proliferate that agony beyond the dark little spaces? Beginning from the observation that photography is an event that fits well within the temporality of politics' immediate object-spectator dialectics,[2] I want to raise a few questions: How does this recording, representation, as well as the act of representing, effect the variety of ways we come to talk, see, and represent what comes under the term of violence, and also what is understood to be pornography?; What kind of sensibilities are summoned, structured, negotiated, sensitized or anesthetized when these terms are evoked and scenes represented? What kind of historicities do they embody and enact and how are they thought and played upon racist and homophobic fields and tropes in our contemporary conditions? These questions being so big, they might as well be put into rooms where police batons are dipped in shoe wax, where images and words are recorded and disseminated.

How is it possible to register an act that is so obscene, and still adopt a critical position so as not to play the same old tunes in which pornographic enactment is understood to empty our gaze and titillate our own attachments to power? And how can we avoid adopting a moralizing discourse of anti-pornography that accepts sex (and violence) only in certain (authorized) doses, leaving intact only "acceptable" sensibilities, and considering pornography as a visual field in which to dig for moral questions—in which overly explicit, repetitive, fantastic, or different displays of sexuality are understood to be pornography? This is a space where pornography not only reflects social and gender inequalities and the

---

2 Ariella Azoulay, *Civil Imagination: Political Ontology of Photography* (London: Verso, 2012)

violence within them, but makes those consuming it enact them in real life. Images from Abu Ghraib and Guantánamo — from empire's circular institutions — have consistently been framed as pornography. A naked Iraqi prisoner on a leash held by an American woman soldier or a bunch of prisoners one on top of another exposing their anuses. As Anne McClintock has persuasively elicited, it is seen, in the utterances of public opinion, as much as in writing by left-wing intellectuals, as an emulation of s/M practices, where internet porno-philes are enacting a state-possessed fantasy of global domination as torture upon the ultimate enemy.[3] In a less self-preoccupied voice she points out that such rendition flattens pornography into a moralistic tale, disregarding the complex dynamics of sexuality, race, class, and gender embedded within these locales and turning the question of "other's torture" into an inquiry about "our morality" thus making the "other's pain" and the historicity of post-colonial cruelty irrelevant.

Beginning from this sober insight and proceeding to the obscenity of the news, it becomes clear that thinking of pornography and violence as inextricably linked would conflate pleasure and pain, power and sexuality, into a singular register and it is also clear that turning such a register into an organizing principle to think about the issue would lead to the same set of impasses and indistinctions as anti-pornographic discourse itself. Similarly, arguing that there is a direct relation between the police baton, as a phallic symbol of law, and an act of penetration, as a scene of domination where the perverse pleasure is power, would move into the vocabulary of psychoanalysis which engages with the structures of the modern subject itself. Yet it is this very coincidence and the conflation of pornography and violence that necessitates our inquiry, requiring these terms to be brought onto a scene where violent and pornographic, phallic and modern, congeal in their political trajectories and genealogies.

---

[3] Anne McClintock, "Paranoid Empire: Specters from Guantánamo and Abu Ghraib," *Small Axe* 13, no. 28 (2009): 50–74.

Dalaev was torturing me with pliers, squeezing my genitals, hitting my toes with the bottle. Nurgaliev was threatening that if I did not give testimony the way they needed it, he would rape me with the police baton. There was a camera that I could see, they were filming me, and also there was a machine that they used to torture me with electricity, there were men in masks with police batons. One of them was telling me that he would rape me with the baton, and they repeated this several times, each of them wanted to do it and they were asking Nurgaliev to allow them to rape me and to record it on video to spread it across the villages. When they were telling me this, I was laying on the floor. Then they picked me up and put me on the table on my belly. A few of them were holding my hands, the others were holding my legs. Nurgaliev said "let's do it, because he does not understand us." They brought some documents and I signed.

The image of crucifixion, for instance, a public act of torture in which so many take pleasure and delight, has been informing our sensibilities for the last couple of thousand years. Modalities of pain and pleasure, as Sade and Masoch represented (the absolute institution of force in sadism and the contractual relation in masochism) already prefigure attitudes and practices towards sexuality and body, the modality of modern power. As Talal Asad has pointed out, the secular body has been constituted, sensitized, and disciplined by religious discourses of transgression and punishment, redemption and horror, empathy and gratification. Accordingly, conceptions of pain and sexuality sedimented in our bodies consistently authorize and organize our attitudes and sensibilities, render certain kinds of sexual acts permissible, certain depictions of pain acceptable while making others transgressive and punishable.[4]

Within this genealogy are the exact instruments and technologies at stake. Handcuffs, dildos, belts, and leg spreaders devised in the nineteenth century to control deviant sexual practices often also created deviancy; they were appropriated by s/M practitioners

---

4   Talal Asad, "Thinking about the Secular Body, Pain, and Liberal Politics," *Cultural Anthropology* 26, no. 4 (2011): 657–675.

to produce pleasure in performative acts that, in a way, exhibited the same power relations as the society that was inventing these tools. Post-porn practitioners and theoreticians took this point further to expropriate the dildo as a de-subjectification technology to displace heteronormative regimes.[5] The dildo not only repeats or embodies the sign of the phallic order (and in the same gesture the very concept of law as embedded in such order espoused by psychoanalysis), but at the same time also deposes the phallus as singular site of pleasure; it is the prosthesis, the machine of desire with no permanent social dynamics, sex or gender position that produces pleasures without being bound to the single subject or bodily part. Katja Diefenbach, reading Preciado through a Marxian understanding of the commodification of bodies, writes:

> The dildo thereby becomes a type of fetish that is no longer a substitute, which does not conceal the abject, which is not affected by a logic of lack, which instead introduces one to the intensities of becoming an interpassive, nameless thing that fucks and is fucked. In this way the dildo not only betrays distribution into living subjects and dead things; it also betrays the socially codified exchange relation between the one who desires and the one who is desired, therefore incorporating desire.[6]

The anus, a non-reproductive, de-sexed zone, the site of pure waste and social taboos, works alongside a dildo to shift the zone of pleasure away from the discursive thralls of vagina or penis. The black hole and the inorganic object, de-socializing the conventionalities of a sexual act, re-appropriating technology rather than opposing and structurally reinforcing it through the fantasy of natural sex or authorized pornography. Desire no longer depends on the subject that's constantly lacking and on the discourse of truth that regiments sexuality, but multiplies and reproduces itself in the

---

[5] Tim Stüttgen (ed.), *Post Porn Politics* (Berlin: b_books, 2009)
[6] Katja Diefenbach, "Fizzle Out in White: Postporn Politics and the Deconstruction of Fetishism," in *Post Porn Politics*, 25–32, at 19.

inter-relational and de-subjectified zone of pleasure and pain. It is a practice that merges and fuses into representational art forms, cinematic experiments, through digital and social media, which ultimately work within forms of representation that are well aware of the limits that they have as resistance to the aesthetic regimes under which they function.

How we can bring these lessons of de-subjectification into different histories of power and the subject, into these scenes which contract body, sexuality, and power in a singular instant, is a serious question, that requires a separate pause. It is highly important to remain sensitive to the histories of particular places with their own stories of body, sex, and representation, without falling into affirmative possibilities of out of place heteronormative sexualities, finding language that would refigure post-porn critique within the subject's body and voice. This move would bring us to the question of representation, or rather to the politics of aesthetics. And here of course, the question is how we can represent that which — in its displacement of intimacy, otherness, in-your-faceness, in its inequality of translation, destruction of trauma — is, we could say, radically unrepresentable. Could reiteration of the scene, replication of the words, the images with all their minutia, would get us in and out of an image of other as a subject without repeating the moralistic tale or affirmative liberation fantasies.

A dancing hall. Such was the picture. Our cell was like a menagerie, they would come and pick some of us. For them it was fun and for us such pain. Each was more cruel than the other, like this Tatarian who chopped Movsar's leg with an axe so that everyone would be afraid of him. Once they put him down badly. Made him eat his own shit. Igor was the chief of detention facilities, and the other one was Sergei. They would torture people together. And there was a barbed wire. They would penetrate us with the barbed wire, I told you, they would put the barbed wire into the tube, and stick it into the ass and then would take out the tube. But the barbed wire would stay. Whatever they wanted. Then try to get this wire out.

Exposition, reiteration of the obscene, the scene overexposed, reality in all its detail, is too much, but too little at the same time. If one repeats words from these scenes (the names of the police batons, in the language of those who are retelling, in the historicity of the acronyms, in the nakedness of an open body), what comes about to the producer of the images (in voice) to the reader of the texts? I am asking: what kind of regime of representation does the repetition of banality of violence and the obscene include? Rancière has persuasively argued that until the mid-nineteenth century, pictorial arts were explicitly dependent on words to elicit invisible presences and meanings in images, and words in literature or poetry constituted images that could produce visibility by regulating the exposure and concealment of meaning according to given sensibilities. In contrast, the aesthetic regime of modernity where the visible and sayable no longer hold determinable relations is concerned with producing a reality of pure presences.[7] These art forms and images do not simply aim to represent certain aspects of life, but also to speak (or stay silent) by themselves. Yet as Rancière explains: "Presence is not the nakedness of the pictorial thing as opposed to the significations of representation. Presence and representation are two regimes of the plaiting of words and forms."[8] Such production still depends in a peculiar way on the visible and sayable (and so too the invisible and unthinkable) being enabled in the presentation. If the invisible or unsayable were once contingent upon the modalities of the representative regime itself and could be modified (artistically), either to render visible and sayable what had been absences, or to retain or make them hidden and unspoken, the modern aesthetic regime of presentation, assuming that things could "speak" for themselves and press their qualities qua pure beings, maintains that such "things" are always in excess of the means of artistic expression and thought. The regime re-constitutes such excess as the unrepresentable and puts it back into the materiality of things while persistently and dramatically speaking and visualizing the "unthinkable" and "unrepresentable"

---

7   Jacques Rancière, *The Future of the Image,* trans. G. Elliot (London: Verso, 2007), 39–43.
8   Ibid., 79.

as a matter of ontological condition, rather than a modality of particular representation. If we consider this tension between radical non-representability and present visuality at work in the scenes that we have presented here, could the catatonic repetition of the obscene, and the relation between the pornographic and scenographic, be reimagined and rethought?

BIOGRAPHIES

Namita Aavriti is a writer, media-maker, researcher in law, technology, culture studies. She works with Pad.ma (Public Access Digital Media Archive) and has worked with Alternative Law Forum for ten years. Her current research interests are the intersections of law, science, technology, and popular culture, and the history of social movements in India. She divides her time between forgetting most of the minutiae of her legal education and relearning the law as ridiculous metaphor and endless archive of stories. She is cis-gender, upper caste, and middle class, and lives in Bangalore.

Eirini Avramopoulou is currently a A.G. Leventis Fellow at the British School at Athens, working on a research project titled "Changing spaces of refugee. Histories and geographies of displacement amidst politics of crisis in Greece." She received a PhD in Social Anthropology from the University of Cambridge (title: "The Affective Language of Activism: An Ethnography of Human Rights, Gender Politics and Activist Coalitions in Istanbul, Turkey", 2012). Her work has been published in several edited volumes and journals, including *The Greek Review of Social Research, Cultural Anthropology/Hot Spots, Critical Interdisciplinarity (Kritiki Diepistimonikotita),* and *Thesis.* Her research interests include anthropology of human rights, social movements, and activism; gender and sexuality; secularism and Islam; queer theory, feminist and psychoanalytic approaches to subjectivity, biopolitics and affect; economic crisis, memory, and trauma. In 2013–2014 she was a fellow at the Institute for Cultural Inquiry (ICI), Berlin and in 2014-2015 she worked as a research fellow at the Sociology Department of the University of Cambridge. At the moment she is completing her first monograph on affect, performativity, and gender-queer activism in Istanbul, Turkey.

Elia Charidi is a PhD candidate of the department of Social Anthropology of Panteion University of Social and Political Sciences in Athens. In her treatise, she elaborates how the subjectivity of blind people and people with visual impairments is constructed in contexts where the sense of vision is privileged as the most objective means for accessing truth, knowledge and aesthetic pleasure. She has published a book review about disability and museums in *Parallax* (vol. 17, no. 3, 2011) and an article in *Levga* (vol. 9, 2012) about disability and social benefits in the Greek context.

Kathryn Fischer a.k.a. Mad Kate is a Berlin based writer and performance artist. Her life-long questions around gender and sexuality have taken her from women's farming cooperatives in Nicaragua to immigration offices in San Francisco to stages in China to queer porn sets in Berlin. A consummate mover, performer, thinker, and writer, she follows her body where it leads. www.alfabus.us

Sinan Goknur is a practice-based PhD student at Duke University's Visual and Media Studies program. Prior to coming to the US, Sinan worked as a volunteer organizer in Lambda Istanbul, and as an administrative staff for Women for Women's Human Rights (WWHR) – New Ways as well as the Coalition for Sexual and Bodily Rights in Muslim Societies (CSBR). In addition to gender and sexuality, Sinan's interests include contemporary art theory, modernity/coloniality critique, global epistemologies of resistance, and critical technology studies.

Graduate of the Beaux Arts and the Ecole Nationale Supérieure de la Photographie, **Émilie Jouvet** is a film director and photographer. She's been exploring the European queer scene for over fifteen years, her photographic work encompassing intimate portraits and subversive mise-en-scène. In 2005 she made her first French, queer porn, lesbian, and transgender feature film: *One*

Night Stand. In 2009 she created an evanescent group of performers, for a unique European tour, with the intention of shooting her second feature film: *Too Much Pussy! Feminist Sluts in the Queer X Show*. A feminist, sex-positive documentary road-movie, released in cinemas across Europe in 2011. She is a member of Oui Oui Oui Egalité, AJL the Association of LGBT journalists and SAFE LGBT, the Association for the fight against violence within the LGBT community. She lives and works between Paris, Marseille, and Brussels.

Mantas Kvedaravicius teaches visual cultures and critical theory in Vilnius University and is conducting a long-term film project in Athens, Istanbul, and Odessa. He holds a PhD in social anthropology from the University of Cambridge and has standing academic and cinematic interests in absence, materiality, and body in their performative and political manifestations. His previous project concentrated on disappearances and dreams in Chechnya and resulted in an award winning documentary essay, "Barzakh."

Irene Peano is a precarious militant researcher. She just completed a two-year Marie Curie Postdoctoral Fellowship at the University of Bologna, where she currently holds another postdoctoral position. Her research project deals with forms of resistance to the regime of mobility control and the exploitation of migrant labour, with a special focus on the agro-industrial context and on its reproductive articulations. She received her PhD from the Department of Social Anthropology at the University of Cambridge, for a project on the bonded sexual labor of Nigerian migrants. Her work focuses on subjectivity, and on the analysis of different forms of power, resistance and escape, with a special focus on gender, sexuality, and affective and reproductive labor.

Eliza Steinbock (Assistant Professor, Department of Film & Literary Studies, Leiden University) writes on contemporary philosophies of the body, visual culture and transfeminist issues. She is an American who completed my Masters (with distinction) in Cultural Studies at the University of Leeds (2004) and Doctorate in Cultural Analysis at the University of Amsterdam ("Shimmering

Images: On Transgender Embodiment and Cinematic Aesthetics" 2011). Her current research project, "Vital Art: Transgender Portraiture as Visual Activism", examines the worlds created in the visual arts to harbor at risk trans subjects and to critique their discrimination. She speaks regularly on aesthetics, sexuality, and transgender studies. Her recent publications include essays in the *Journal of Homosexuality, Photography and Culture,* and TSQ: *Transgender Studies Quarterly.* Please visit www.elizasteinbock.com for more information.

Graduated in South Asian Studies at Cambridge University and in Screen Documentary at Goldsmiths, **Adele Tulli** today works as a documentary filmmaker and film programmer. She has directed award-winning films such as *365 without 377,* about the decriminalization of homosexuality in India, and Rebel Menopause, the intimate portrait of Thérèse Clerc and her inspiring ideas on aging as a "time of complete freedom." She is currently doing a practice-based PhD in film at the Roehampton University in London and she is the programmer of CinemaItaliaUk, the monthly event that brings the best contemporary Italian cinema to London.

www.ingramcontent.com/pod-product-compliance
Lightning Source LLC
Chambersburg PA
CBHW070849160426

43192CB00012B/2366